I0015480

Mastering System Center Configuration Manager

Master how to configure, back up, and secure
access to System Center Configuration Manager
with this practical guide

Vangel Krstevski

BIRMINGHAM - MUMBAI

Mastering System Center Configuration Manager

Copyright © 2014 Packt Publishing

All rights reserved. No part of this book may be reproduced, stored in a retrieval system, or transmitted in any form or by any means, without the prior written permission of the publisher, except in the case of brief quotations embedded in critical articles or reviews.

Every effort has been made in the preparation of this book to ensure the accuracy of the information presented. However, the information contained in this book is sold without warranty, either express or implied. Neither the author, nor Packt Publishing, and its dealers and distributors will be held liable for any damages caused or alleged to be caused directly or indirectly by this book.

Packt Publishing has endeavored to provide trademark information about all of the companies and products mentioned in this book by the appropriate use of capitals. However, Packt Publishing cannot guarantee the accuracy of this information.

First published: December 2014

Production reference: 1191214

Published by Packt Publishing Ltd.
Livery Place
35 Livery Street
Birmingham B3 2PB, UK.

ISBN 978-1-78217-545-2

www.packtpub.com

Credits

Author

Vangel Krstevski

Reviewers

Deepak Agarwal

Roel van Bueren

Torsten Meringer

Stephen Carter

Commissioning Editor

Amarabha Banerjee

Acquisition Editor

Subho Gupta

Content Development Editor

Athira Laji

Technical Editors

Shubhangi Dhamgaye

Humera Shaikh

Copy Editors

Dipti Kapadia

Deepa Nambiar

Project Coordinator

Harshal Ved

Proofreaders

Simran Bhogal

Paul Hindle

Maria Gould

Ameesha Green

Indexer

Rekha Nair

Production Coordinator

Conidon Miranda

Cover Work

Conidon Miranda

About the Author

Vangel Krstevski is an IT engineer with 5 years of experience in engineering IT Systems based on Microsoft guidelines. He is a strong team player with an affinity for details. His strengths include excellent communication skills, hands-on experience with various Microsoft products, and the ability to manage conflicts and accomplish demands to the agreed standards and timelines. He is currently employed by Re-Aktiv, a software development and consultancy company from Skopje, Macedonia, which specializes in the area of electronic services and company public registry solutions. His main areas of expertise are server virtualization, hybrid cloud scenario design and implementation, and Business Continuity along with System Center. He has worked on many projects, both internal and commercial, as a consultant for Microsoft server-side platforms. He has already written a book titled *Hyper-V Replica Essentials*, *Packt Publishing*, which helps organizations to implement business continuity and disaster recovery strategies.

I would like to thank my family, friends, and colleagues for supporting me, especially my girlfriend, Monika, who stood by me and gave me support and motivation during the process of writing of this book.

About the Reviewers

Deepak Agarwal [Microsoft MVP] is a Microsoft Certified Professional who has been working professionally on Dynamics AX. He has worked with different versions of Axapta, such as AX 2009, AX 2012, R2, and R3. He has held a wide range of development, consulting, and leading roles while always maintaining the role of a business application developer. Although his strengths are rooted in X++ development, he is a highly regarded developer and has an extensive knowledge of the technical aspects of Dynamics AX development and customization.

He was awarded the title of Most Valuable Professional (MVP) on Dynamics AX in 2013 and 2014 by Microsoft. He has also worked on *Microsoft Dynamics AX 2012 Reporting Cookbook, Packt Publishing*, and is currently reviewing two more books, both for Packt Publishing.

Deepak shares his experience with Dynamics AX on his blog at `http://theaxapta.blogspot.in/`.

A big thanks to my dear friends Chetan Sharma and Chetan Tanwar for their motivation, support, and guidance.

Roel van Bueren works as the Chief Architect and Product Director for ROVABU Software BV. Roel specializes in software packaging using Windows Installer, OS Deployment (OSD), and Electronic Software Distribution (ESD) using Microsoft System Center Configuration Manager, Novell ZENworks Configuration Management, RES Automation Manager, and ENGL Imaging Toolkit. His latest projects involve Bundle Commander for Novell ZENworks Configuration Management and Setup Commander for Microsoft System Center Configuration Manager 2012, Microsoft Deployment Toolkit, and other ESD solutions, such as Dell KACE and RES Automation Manager.

Torsten Meringer is a ConfigMgr MVP since 2005 and is a self-employed senior consultant located in Germany. He started his own business in 1999 and primarily focusses on designing, migrating, deploying, training, automating, and troubleshooting Microsoft's deployment and management solutions, such as System Center Configuration Manager, System Center Orchestrator, and Microsoft Deployment Toolkit in small-scale to large-scale companies ranging from 500 to more than 200,000 clients. Torsten manages the German ConfigMgr blog, `http://www.mssccmfaq.de`, and holds various MCT, MCSA, MCSE, MCTS, and MCITP:EA certifications. He is also an author and often speaks at various Microsoft events.

Stephen Carter is a successful, independent IT consultant who specializes in infrastructure automation. He has over 20 years of experience in the IT industry and has been working with Microsoft's Configuration Management solutions since SMS 2003. He has designed, implemented, deployed, and developed Configuration Management infrastructures for a number of global financial institutions.

He is passionate about automation and has spent a large part of his career in streamlining and developing innovative solutions to assist his clients with simplifying their IT processes.

Originally from the UK, Stephen now lives in Australia with his wife and three children.

www.PacktPub.com

Support files, eBooks, discount offers, and more

For support files and downloads related to your book, please visit www.PacktPub.com.

Did you know that Packt offers eBook versions of every book published, with PDF and ePub files available? You can upgrade to the eBook version at www.PacktPub.com and as a print book customer, you are entitled to a discount on the eBook copy. Get in touch with us at service@packtpub.com for more details.

At www.PacktPub.com, you can also read a collection of free technical articles, sign up for a range of free newsletters and receive exclusive discounts and offers on Packt books and eBooks.

https://www2.packtpub.com/books/subscription/packtlib

Do you need instant solutions to your IT questions? PacktLib is Packt's online digital book library. Here, you can search, access, and read Packt's entire library of books.

Why subscribe?
- Fully searchable across every book published by Packt
- Copy and paste, print, and bookmark content
- On demand and accessible via a web browser

Free access for Packt account holders

If you have an account with Packt at www.PacktPub.com, you can use this to access PacktLib today and view 9 entirely free books. Simply use your login credentials for immediate access.

Instant updates on new Packt books

Get notified! Find out when new books are published by following @PacktEnterprise on Twitter or the *Packt Enterprise* Facebook page.

Table of Contents

Preface

Microsoft System Center Configuration Manager is a powerful System Management product that helps IT administrators with better asset management and organization by grouping them into logical containers. These logical containers allow you to make the deployment of applications easier, software and security updates, antimalware definitions, and so on. Configuration Manager assists you in operating system deployment, allowing you to deploy OS images to multiple target systems at the same time. It also empowers users to be more productive from anywhere on any device by implementing state-of-the-art mobile device management functionalities.

What this book covers

Chapter 1, Introduction to System Center Configuration Manager 2012 R2, is all about the initial setup of Configuration Manager 2012 R2. It shows you how to install and set up all the prerequisites and requirements. In the end, there is an explanation on System Center Configuration Manager sites and site hierarchy and all of the site features and functionalities.

Chapter 2, Assets and Compliance, is more about compliance settings and Endpoint Protection. Compliance settings, with knowledge and creativity, can give you feedback about the configuration and compliance of your Windows-based systems and mobile devices.

Chapter 3, The Software Library, explains the different ways in which you can deploy software and also explains how you can use System Center Configuration Manager to do this. It gives you an overview of what applications are and how to create them in Configuration Manager, how to make deployment types, and how to create different detection rules.

Chapter 4, Reporting in Configuration Manager, explains how SQL Server Reporting Services give you the opportunity to show the information contained in the Configuration manager database using SSRS reporting.

Chapter 5, Administration and Monitoring, describes the way in which the System Center Configuration Manager hierarchy is organized. Towards the end, it discusses all the aspects of client settings and how to use these settings to make an optimal configuration for your business needs.

Chapter 6, Cloud Integration, describes the benefits of a public cloud, specifically Windows Azure, and explains how you can use System Center Configuration Manager 2012 R2 to deliver application packages to your clients that run on different mobile device operating systems.

Chapter 7, Security and Backup, describes the infrastructure security for Configuration Manager and the delegation of administrative access. This chapter includes a detailed description of a new role-based administration model and an overview of the Configuration Manager controls and security accounts.

Chapter 8, Troubleshooting, presents the different aspects of how to troubleshoot issues related to the functionalities of Configuration Manager. It begins with common network-related issues and continues by explaining common Configuration Manager console issues.

What you need for this book

In order to be able to follow the guidelines in this book and implement the procedures explained in it, you will need the following software:

- System Center Configuration Manager 2012 R2
- Microsoft Windows Server 2012 R2
- 7 ZIP
- Microsoft SQL Server Report Builder 2012
- Windows Azure

Who this book is for

This book is excellent for IT administrators who want to improve their system and asset management. A fair understanding of the core elements and applications related to SCCM will be helpful.

Conventions

In this book, you will find a number of styles of text that distinguish between different kinds of information. Here are some examples of these styles, and an explanation of their meaning.

Code words in text, database table names, folder names, filenames, file extensions, pathnames, dummy URLs, user input, and Twitter handles are shown as follows: "You can use the prerequisites checker tool that is provided with the System Center Configuration Manager 2012 R2 installation media, which is located in `\SMSSETUP\BIN\x64\prereqchk.exe`."

A block of code is set as follows:

```
mpcmdrun.exe -removedefinitions [All]
```

Any command-line input or output is written as follows:

```
SMSEP Setup Started....
Installing the SMSEP
Unable to query registry key
(SOFTWARE\Microsoft\Windows\CurrentVersion\Uninstall\Microsoft Security Client),
return (0x00000002) means EP client is NOT installed
Installation was successful.
```

New terms and **important words** are shown in bold. Words that you see on the screen, in menus or dialog boxes for example, appear in the text like this: "To view or edit the configuration items on a particular site, click on the **Assets and Compliance** section of the Configuration Manager console and select **Compliance Settings**."

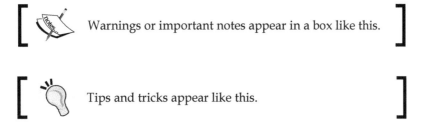

Warnings or important notes appear in a box like this.

Tips and tricks appear like this.

Reader feedback

Feedback from our readers is always welcome. Let us know what you think about this book—what you liked or may have disliked. Reader feedback is important for us to develop titles that you really get the most out of.

To send us general feedback, simply send an e-mail to feedback@packtpub.com, and mention the book title via the subject of your message.

If there is a topic that you have expertise in and you are interested in either writing or contributing to a book, see our author guide on www.packtpub.com/authors.

Customer support

Now that you are the proud owner of a Packt book, we have a number of things to help you to get the most from your purchase.

Errata

Although we have taken every care to ensure the accuracy of our content, mistakes do happen. If you find a mistake in one of our books—maybe a mistake in the text or the code—we would be grateful if you would report this to us. By doing so, you can save other readers from frustration and help us improve subsequent versions of this book. If you find any errata, please report them by visiting http://www.packtpub.com/submit-errata, selecting your book, clicking on the **errata submission form** link, and entering the details of your errata. Once your errata are verified, your submission will be accepted and the errata will be uploaded on our website, or added to any list of existing errata, under the Errata section of that title. Any existing errata can be viewed by selecting your title from http://www.packtpub.com/support.

Piracy

Piracy of copyright material on the Internet is an ongoing problem across all media. At Packt, we take the protection of our copyright and licenses very seriously. If you come across any illegal copies of our works, in any form, on the Internet, please provide us with the location address or website name immediately so that we can pursue a remedy.

Please contact us at copyright@packtpub.com with a link to the suspected pirated material.

We appreciate your help in protecting our authors, and our ability to bring you valuable content.

Questions

You can contact us at questions@packtpub.com if you are having a problem with any aspect of the book, and we will do our best to address it.

1
Introduction to System Center Configuration Manager 2012 R2

System Center Configuration Manager, formerly named Systems Management Server, is a Microsoft product that is a part of the System Center Suite. It provides management capabilities for large groups of different device types such as workstations, servers, laptops, and mobile devices. These devices can run on different operating systems such as Windows, Windows Embedded, Linux, UNIX, Mac OS X, Windows Phone, iOS, Symbian OS, and Android. Not only does it provide management of such device types, but it also provides these features: remote control for some of the devices' OSes, software distribution, patches and patch management, operating system deployment, and creating devices' software and hardware inventory. So, System Center Configuration Manager provides both efficient and effective IT services with the help of scalable software deployment, devices compliance management, as well as the asset management of discovered hardware and software resources.

System Center Configuration Manager helps with the control of its IT infrastructure and assets. The asset management functionality provides IT engineers with a detailed image of the software and hardware inventory, which clients are using them, and where they are located in the infrastructure. This asset management functionality provides reports that help enterprises to optimize their hardware and software usage and take better strategic decisions regarding software licenses and compliance with these licenses.

System Center Configuration Manager 2012 R2 – requirements

System Center Configuration Manager has multiple requirements that you need to take into consideration before executing any deployment of System Center Configuration Manager 2012 R2. The following are the requirements:

- Site systems cannot be installed on Server Core installations for the following operating systems:
  - Windows Server 2008 or Windows Server 2008 R2
  - Windows Server 2008 Foundation or Windows Server 2008 R2 Foundation
  - Windows Server 2012 or Windows Server 2012 R2; an exception to this is that starting with System Center 2012 R2 Configuration Manager, these operating systems support the distribution point site system role, without PXE or multicast support
  - Windows Server 2012 Foundation or Windows Server 2012 R2 Foundation

- After a site system server is installed, you cannot change the following:
  - The domain name of the domain where the site system server is located
  - The domain membership of the server
  - The name of the server

- Configuration Manager Site system roles cannot be installed on an instance of a Windows Server Failover Cluster. You can only install the site database server on Windows Server Failover Cluster.

For the full list of requirements, take a look at the following link:

```
http://technet.microsoft.com/en-us/library/gg682077.aspx#BKMK_
SupConfigSiteSystemReq
```

Prerequisites for System Center Configuration Manager 2012 R2

Before you start deploying System Center Configuration Manager, you must make sure that your infrastructure meets all of the prerequisites. What follows is a list and a step-by-step guide that shows you how to meet these prerequisites.

Creating the System Management container

When the Active Directory schema is extended, the System Management container in Active Directory is not created by default. The container has to be created in all Active Directory domains that contain a primary site server or a secondary site server that publishes site information to Active Directory. In order to create the System Management container, take a look at the following steps:

1. You have to log on to your Domain Controller and open **ADSI Edit**. You can also do this from any other machine that has **ADSI Edit** installed on it and connect to the Domain Controller. The account that you use to connect to the Domain Controller must have permissions to modify objects in **ADSI Edit**. You can open **ADSI Edit** from **Server Manager Console**, from the Control Panel\System and Security\Administrative Tools locations or by opening **Run** under the Start icon and typing adsiedit.msc:

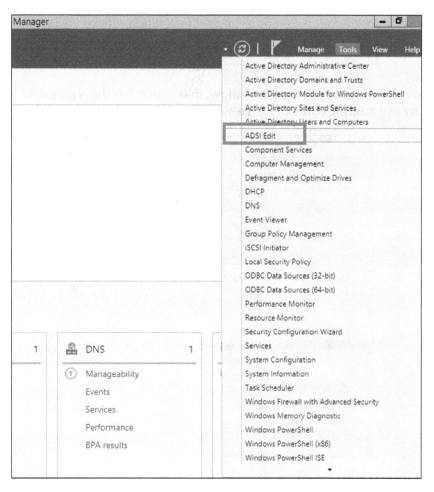

2. Right-click on **ADSI Edit** and click on **Connect to...**:

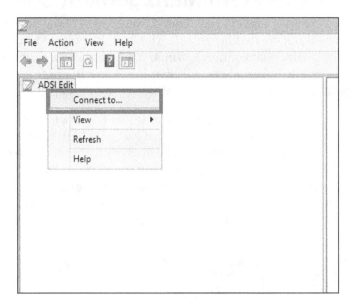

3. In the **Connection Settings** window, make sure that the **Name** field is set to **Default naming context**. Leave everything else as it is and click on **OK**:

4. In the **ADSI Edit** console, expand **Default naming context** in the folder pane, right-click on **CN=System**, click on **New**, and then click on **Object...**:

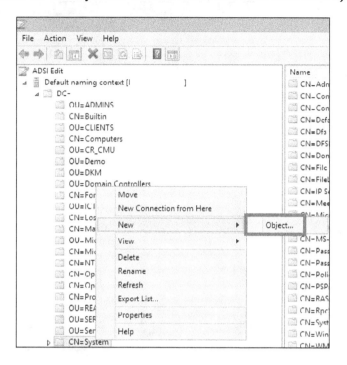

5. When the **Create Object** window appears, select **container** and click on **Next**:

6. Enter System Management in the **Value** textbox and click on **Next** to finish:

With this, the **System Management** container is created in Active Directory. Next, we have to join the site server to the Active Directory domain and give computer account permissions to the site server to publish the site information to the container. A primary site server computer account must have full control permissions on the **System Management** container. To do this, perform the following steps:

1. Open the **Active Directory Users and Computers** console or open **Run** under the Start icon and type dsa.msc.

2. Navigate to the **System Management** container, right-click on it, and select **Delegate Control....** When you click on **Delegate Control...**, a wizard starts, which guides you through the process:

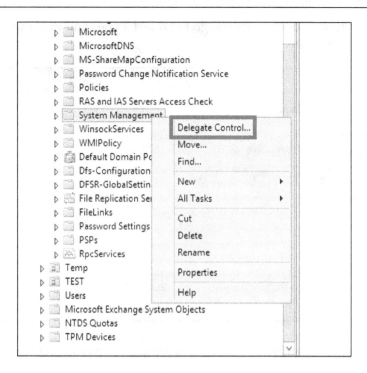

3. In the first window, just click on **Next**.

4. In the second window, click on **Add...**:

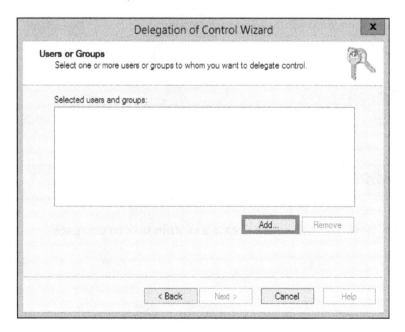

5. When a new window appears, go to **Object Types** and make sure that **Computers** is checked:

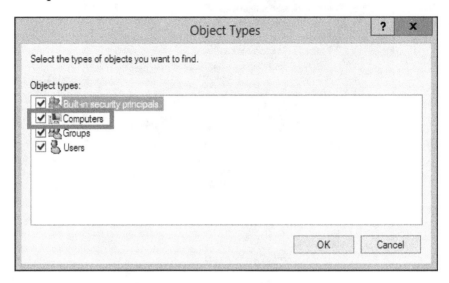

6. Then, add your primary site server's computer account and click on **OK**:

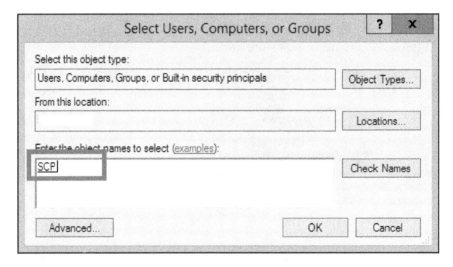

7. In the next window, select **Create a custom task to delegate**:

8. Select **This folder, existing objects in this folder, and creation of new objects in this folder** and click on **Next**:

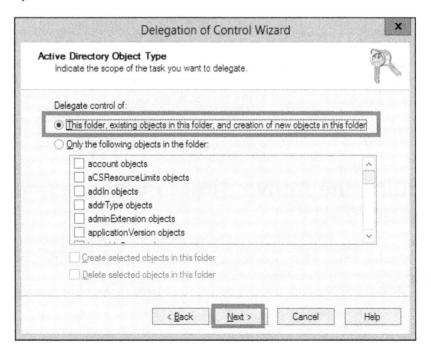

9. In the next window, select all the three options under **Show these permissions** and select **Full Control** under **Permissions**. Then, click on **Next**:

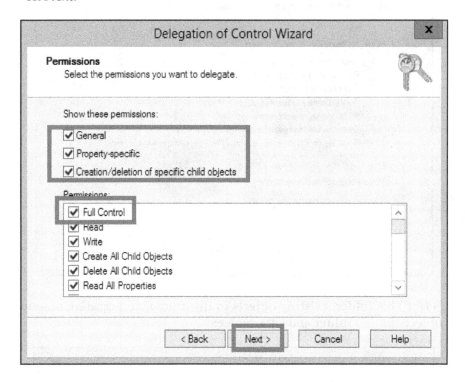

We have now delegated full permissions to the primary site server's computer account on the System Management container. To find out how to create the System Management container in a different way, check this link:

```
https://gallery.technet.microsoft.com/scriptcenter/Create-SCCM-
System-91fee476
```

Extending the Active Directory schema for SCCM 2012 R2

In order to extend the Active Directory Schema for System Center Configuration Manager 2012 R2, you need to use a tool that is located in the installation media of System Center Configuration Manager 2012 R2. You can also use the ldif file. This file will enable you to import or export information to or from Active Directory.

Open the installation media, go to SMSSETUP, then open BIN, and go to x64; you will find **extadsch.exe**. You can either click on this or copy the path and run it from the command prompt. To run `extadsch.exe`, you have to use an account with Schema Admin permissions.

When it finishes, you should see the following message in the command prompt:

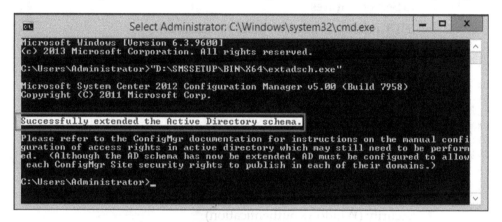

Installing Windows Server's roles and features

Before you can install the required Windows Server roles and features for System Center Configuration Manager 2012 R2, you need to make sure you have done the following:

- Created the System Management container
- Assigned permissions to the primary site server or multiple primary, secondary, and a CAS server
- Extended the Active Directory schema

You can use the prerequisites checker tool that is provided with the System Center Configuration Manager 2012 R2 installation media, which is located in `\SMSSETUP\ BIN\x64\prereqchk.exe`. You can also use PowerShell or the tool from the following link to install all the prerequisites:

`https://gallery.technet.microsoft.com/ConfigMgr-2012-R2-e52919cd`

The following is a list of the Windows Server roles, features, and role services required by System Center Configuration Manager 2012 R2:

- Windows Server role
    - ○ Web Server

- Windows Server features
    - ○ .NET Framework 3.5 (with all subfeatures)
    - ○ .NET Framework 4.5 (with all subfeatures)
    - ○ BITS
    - ○ Remote Differential Compression

- Windows Server role features
    - ○ Common HTTP features (Default Document and Static Content)
    - ○ Application development (ASP.NET 3.5, .NET extensibility 3.5, ASP.NET 4.5, and ISAPI extensions)
    - ○ Security (Windows authentication)
    - ○ IIS 6 Management Compatibility (IIS Management Console, IIS 6 Metabase Compatibility, IIS 6 WMI Compatibility, and IIS Management Scripts and Tools)

Installing ADK 8.1 for SCCM 2012 R2

The Windows **Assessment and Deployment Kit (ADK)** is a set of tools that allow you to customize, assess, and deploy Windows operating systems to new machines. The installation process is simple and straightforward. You can download the ADK from the following location:

```
http://www.microsoft.com/en-US/download/details.aspx?id=39982
```

The only thing that you need to keep in mind is feature selection. Proceed with the following steps:

1. In the first step, choose the **Install Path** tab and click on **Next**:

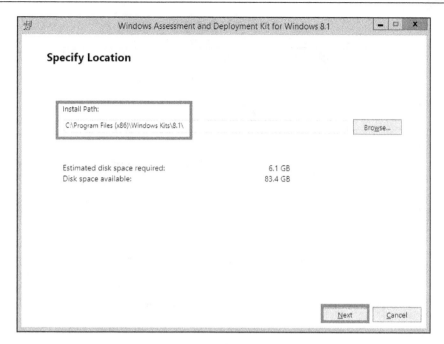

2. Next, select whether you want to join the customer experience improvement program and click on **Next**:

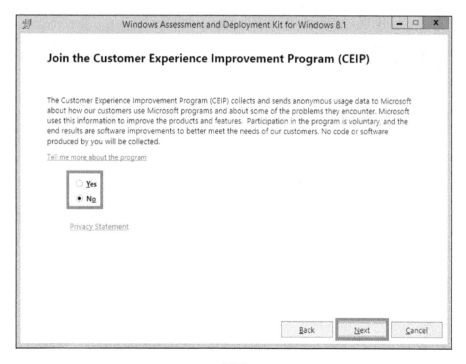

3. Next, you have to accept the license agreement by clicking on **Accept**:

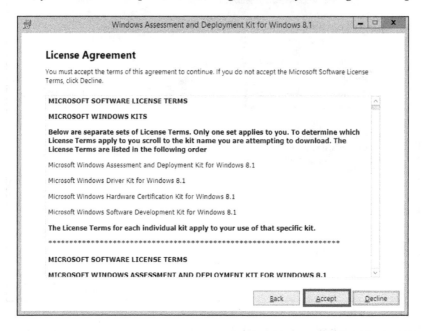

4. Now, you have to choose which of the features should be installed. Only select the ones that are selected in the following screenshot. Click on **Install** to start the installation process:

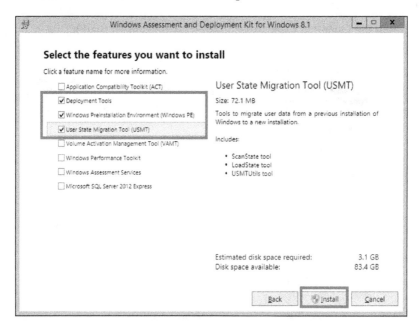

Installing MS SQL Server 2012

After fulfilling all the requirements and installing the prerequisites for System Center Configuration Manager 2012 R2, you need to install MS SQL Server. There are two different deployment scenarios for MS SQL Server. You can deploy it locally, on the same machine as System Center Configuration Manager 2012 R2, or you can deploy it on a remote server. Deploying MS SQL Server locally requires less administration and better performance. Deploying it on a remote server requires specific firewall ports to be opened in order to allow communication between System Center Configuration Manager 2012 R2 and the database server. Use the following link to see which firewall ports need to be open in order for System Center Configuration Manager 2012 R2 to function normally:

`http://technet.microsoft.com/en-us/library/hh427328.aspx`

When you set up MS SQL Server for System Center Configuration Manager and if you choose to go with a remote database server, you need to choose whether you will use Windows Server Failover Clustering. System Center Configuration Manager 2012 R2 cannot be deployed on a Windows Server Failover Cluster, but MS SQL Server can. If you use Windows Server Failover Cluster for the database server, it will give you high availability and resilience in case of an equipment malfunction. This is not a requirement, and it is totally up to you to decide whether to use it or not. Use the following link to see how to create a MS SQL Server failover cluster:

`http://blogs.technet.com/b/meamcs/archive/2013/02/15/sql-2012-failover-cluster-build-step-by-step-part-1-installing-sql-2012.aspx`

For the purpose of the book, I will demonstrate how to install MS SQL Server locally on the server, where later I will install System Center Configuration Manager 2012 R2:

1. Insert the installation media and double-click on it or run the setup.

2. Click on **Installation** from the left-hand side pane and select **New SQL Server stand-alone installation or add features to an existing installation**, as shown in the following screenshot:

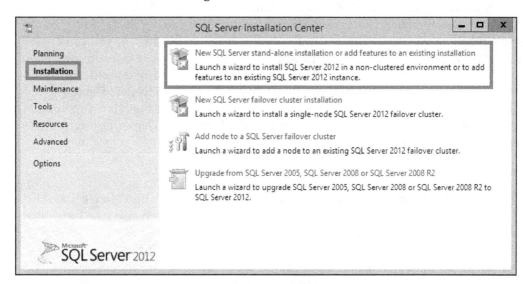

3. Select **I accept the license terms** and click on **Next**:

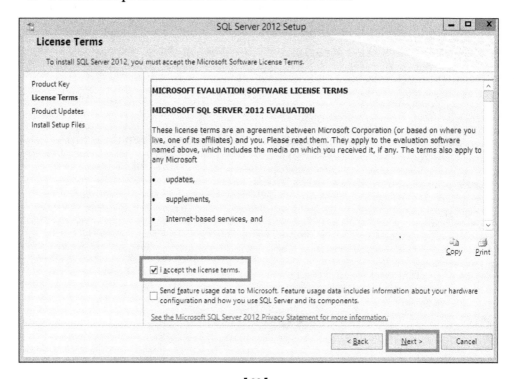

4. After all the rules under **Setup Support Rules** have been checked, click on **Next**:

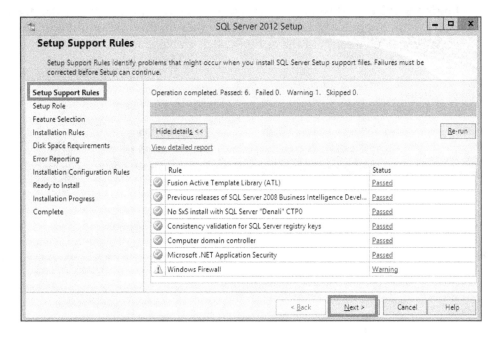

5. In the **Setup Role** window, select **SQL Server Feature Installation** and click on **Next**:

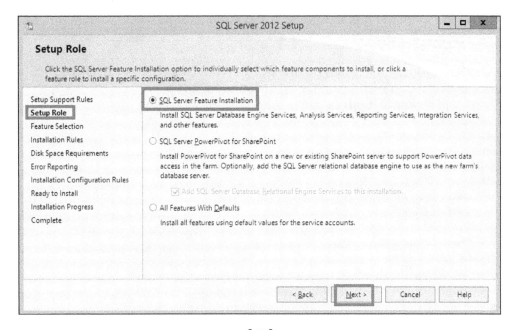

6. In the **Feature Selection** window, select all the features that you will need. System Center Configuration Manager 2012 R2 only requires **Database Engine Services** and **Reporting Services – Native**. You can also install the SQL Management tools so that you can connect to this server and administer it. After you have selected the options, click on **Next**:

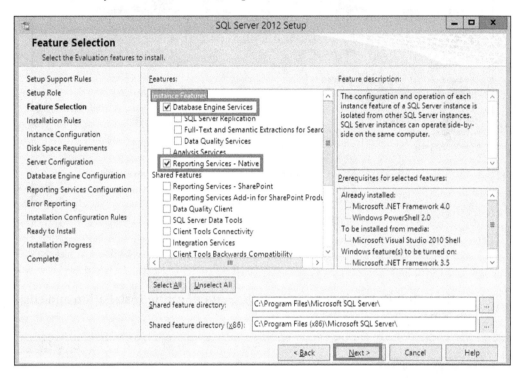

7. Now, you need to configure the SQL Server instance. You can choose between the default or a named instance. For the purpose of the book, I will choose **Default instance**. After this, click on **Next**:

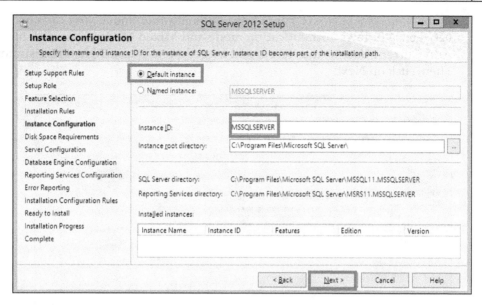

8. In this step, you have to select the run as account for the MS SQL Server Services and the collation. If you are running an English OS, you can use the default collation type; if not, you have to choose another collation type. For the run as account, you can select the default, local accounts, or domain account. After you have input the accounts and their respective passwords, click on **Next**:

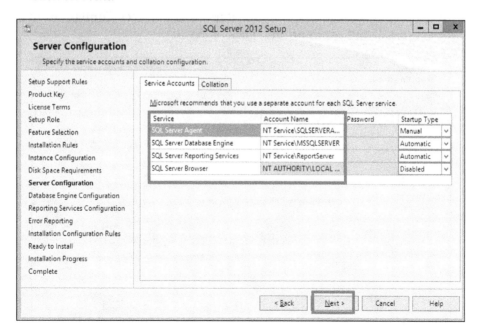

9. In this step, you have to configure the authentication mode. You can choose between **Windows authentication mode** and **Mixed Mode**. Also, click on **Add Current User** to add the current logged-on user as a SQL administrator. Then, click on **Next**:

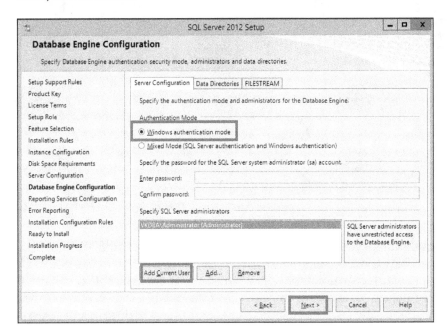

10. In this step, you have to specify the **Reporting Services Configuration** mode. Select **Install and configure** and click on **Next**:

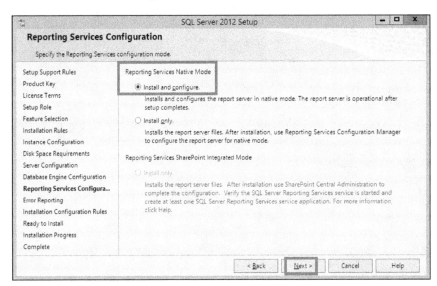

11. The final step is to review all the settings. You can also download and install additional MS SQL Server updates and service packs that are not required. Go through them and click on **Next** to start the installation:

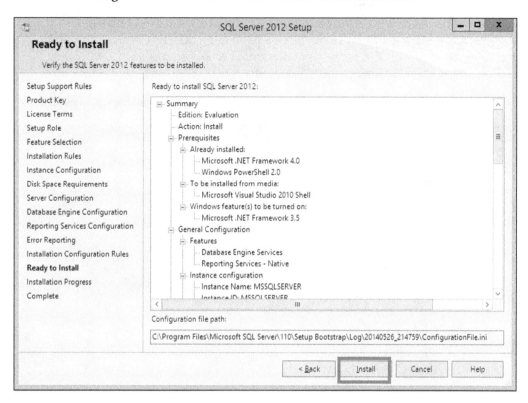

Installing Windows Server Update Services

The final prerequisite for System Center Configuration Manager 2012 R2 is WSUS. This is a standalone product used to distribute updates to systems running the Windows operating system. To install WSUS using a PowerShell command, you have to open PowerShell and type `Install-WindowsFeature -Name UpdateServices-Services, UpdateServices-DB -IncludeManagementTools`.

To use an alternative database server, use the following command:

```
.\wsusutil.exe postinstall SQL_INSTANCE_NAME="servername" CONTENT_
DIR="D:\ WSUS"
```

Installing System Center Configuration Manager 2012 R2

In this section, we will go through the installation process for System Center Configuration Manager 2012 R2. So far, we have gone through the requirements, prerequisites, and MS SQL Server installation. The next step is to install System Center Configuration Manager 2012 R2 itself:

1. Insert the installation media and when the wizard starts, click on **Install**:

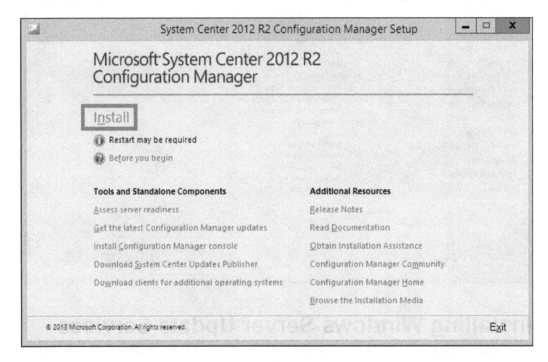

2. Then, just click on **Next**:

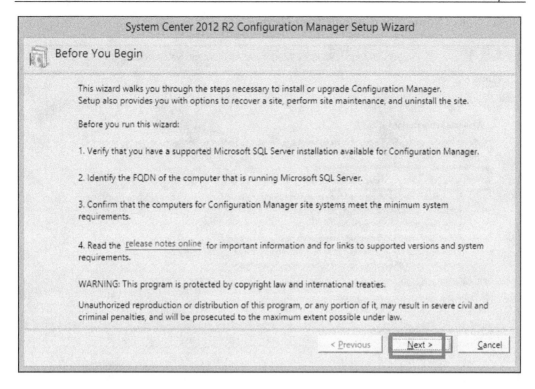

3. Now, you have to choose an option from the **Available Setup Options** window. You can select any one of the following options:

　　○ **Install a Configuration Manager primary site**

　　This is an option for small- and medium-sized organizations that run less than 100,000 clients.

　　○ **Install a Configuration Manager central administration site**

　　This is an option for large organizations that run more than 100,000 clients. You can install a central administration site and have multiple primary sites under it.

4. Select your option and click on **Next**:

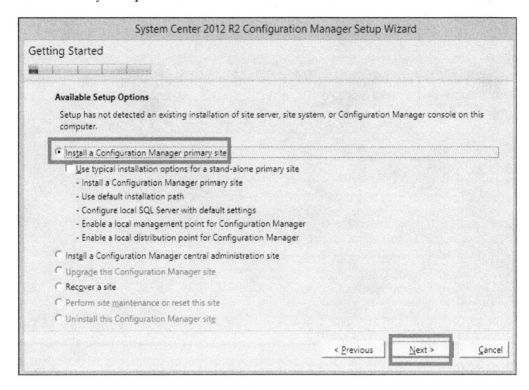

5. Enter your license code and click on **Next**:

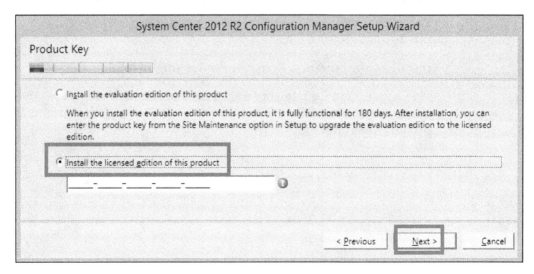

6. Click on **I accept these license terms** and then on **Next**:

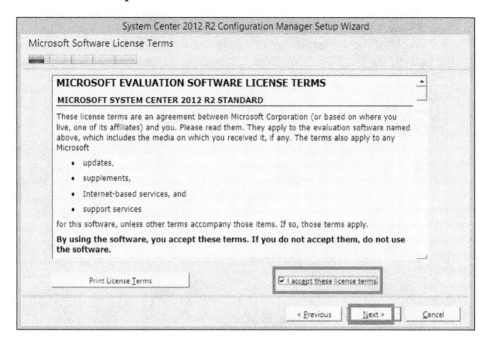

7. Check all the three checkboxes and click on **Next**:

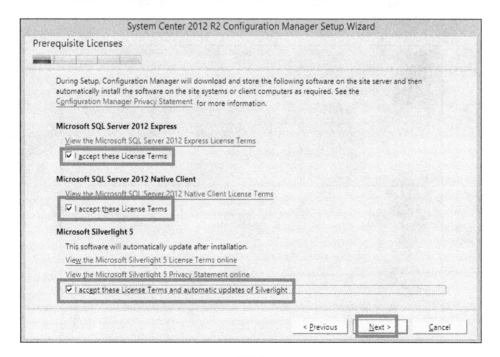

8. In this step, you can either download the required files or use the previously downloaded files. In the *Prerequisites for System Center Configuration Manager 2012 R2* section, two tools have been explained, which can be used to predownload these files. If the files are predownloaded, you have to choose the path to the location of the files. Choose your option and click on **Next**:

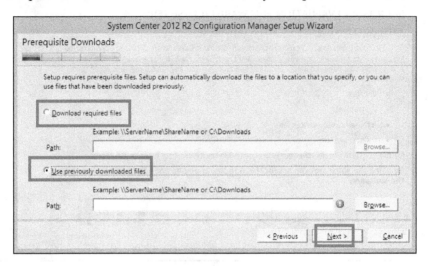

9. In this step, you have to choose the languages you want to install. This will be the language displayed in the System Center Configuration Manager 2012 R2 console and reports:

10. Now, just click on **Next**:

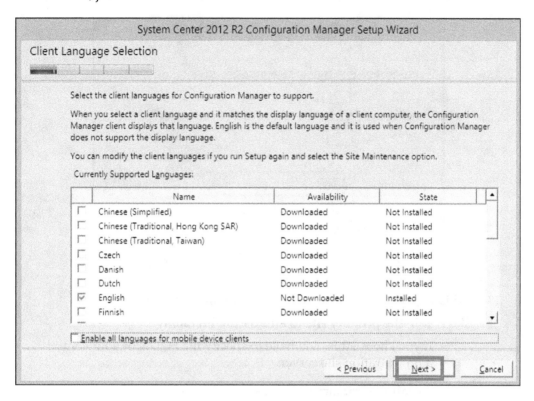

11. In this step, you have to enter values for the following fields:

    ° **Site code**

    This is the code that uniquely identifies your site and can consist of numbers and letters.

    ° **Site name**

    This is the name that uniquely identifies your site.

    ° **Installation folder**

    This is the location of System Center Configuration Manager 2012 R2 in the filesystem. You can find more guidelines on installation folder recommendations for production environments at the following link:

    http://technet.microsoft.com/en-us/library/hh846235.
    aspx#BKMK_ReqDiskSpace

12. Select **Install the Configuration Manager console** and click on **Next**:

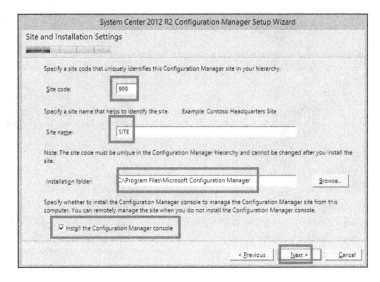

13. In this step, you can choose from the following options:

  ° **Join the primary site to an existing hierarchy**

    If you choose this, you have to specify the FQDN of your central administration site server

  ° **Install the primary site as a stand-alone site**

    Select this if you don't have a central administration site server in your infrastructure:

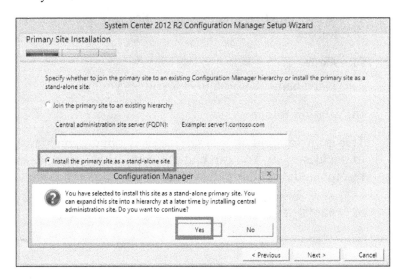

14. In this step, you have to enter your MS SQL Server's name. If you are using MS SQL Server Cluster, enter your MS SQL Server cluster's name for **SQL Server name (FQDN)**. Enter the instance's name and the database's name and click on **Next**:

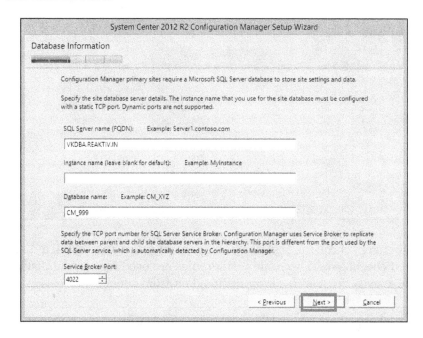

15. In this step, you have to enter your SMS provider (FQDN). The SMS provider is used by the System Center Configuration Manager console and Resource Explorer, and it uses WMI to read and write to the site database. Enter your primary site server's name in the **SMS Provider (FQDN)** field and click on **Next**:

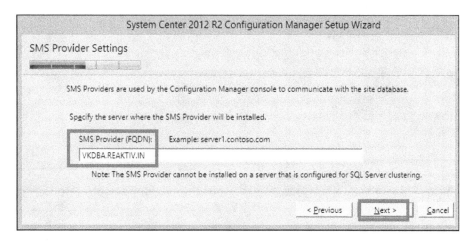

16. In this step, select **Configure the communication method on each site system role** and click on **Next**:

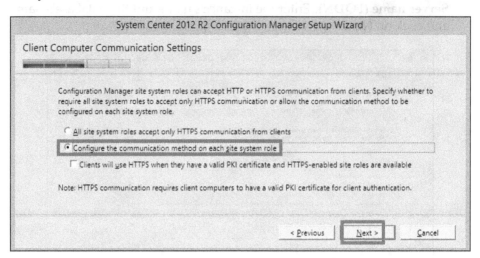

17. In this step, check the **Install a management point** and **Install a distribution point** checkboxes. These site system roles are used for content distribution and management with configuration data from clients:

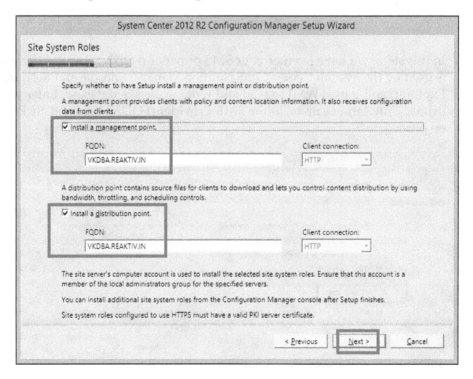

18. Go through all the settings and click on **Next**:

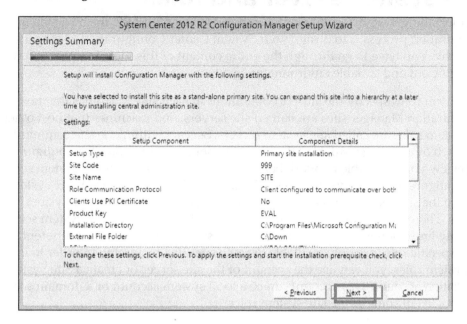

19. Run a prerequisite check, and if it is completed without errors, click on **Begin Install**:

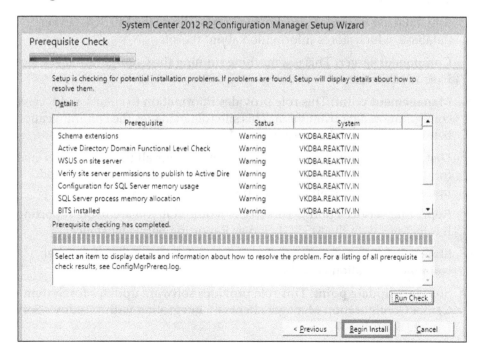

Site system server and roles

After installing System Center Configuration Manager 2012 R2, the next step in the configuration process is to design your System Center Configuration Manager site hierarchy. You have to go through the entire content of this topic in order to have a more efficient and scalable environment.

Site system roles specify the support operations at each site. Machines that host Configuration Manager sites are named site servers, and machines that host other site system roles are called site system servers. Servers within one site communicate with each other using SMB, HTTP, or HTTPS, depending on the site's configuration. So, review your available network bandwidth before installing a site system server and configure your site system roles. Within each site, you can install site system roles on the site server or you can install site system roles on other site system servers. There is no limit to the number of site system roles on a site system server. The only limitation is that you cannot install a site system role from a different site. Some specific roles are only available to some sites in a hierarchy. In order to install site system roles, you can use the account of the site server or create a Site System Installation account. This account can be a local system account or a domain account. Here is a list of some of the site system roles:

- **Site system role**: A machine that provides some of the core functionality for the site. Any machine that hosts a site system role is called a site system server.

- **Site database server**: A site database server hosts the MS SQL Server database, which stores information about the site.

- **Component server**: This is a machine running the Configuration Manager Executive service.

- **Management point**: This role provides information to clients and receives configuration data from them. This site role manages the communication between a client and a site server.

- **Distribution point**: This site system role contains all the source files enabled for download by clients, such as applications, software packages and updates, OS images, and their respective boot images.

- **Reporting services point**: This role is required if you are using reporting. It integrates with the MS SQL Server Reporting Service instance.

- **State migration point**: This role is used to store the user's state when a computer migration is performed.

- **Software update point**: This role provides software updates for System Center Configuration Manager clients by integrating with Windows Server Update Services.

- **System health validator point**: This is a necessary role if you use Configuration Validation performed by Network Access Protection, and it is installed only on a NAP-enabled server.

- **Endpoint Protection point**: This is an optional site system role that Configuration Manager uses to enable Endpoint Protection on your site.

- **Fallback status point**: This role provides an alternative location for clients to send messages to during installation when they cannot reach their management point. This role monitors client installation and identifies clients that are unmanaged because they cannot reach their management point.

- **Out-of-band service point**: This role is used for the provisioning and configuration of Intel AMT-based computers.

- **Asset intelligence synchronization point**: This connects to System Center Online in order to download Asset Intelligence catalog information and upload uncategorized titles so that they can be considered for future inclusion in the catalog.

- **Application Catalog web service point**: This role provides information on the Application Catalog website from Software Library.

- **Application Catalog website point**: This role provides clients with a list of the available software from Application Catalog.

- **Enrollment proxy point**: This role intercepts enrollment requests from mobile devices so that they can be managed by System Center Configuration Manager.

- **Enrollment point**: This role provides PKI certificates to mobile devices to finish the enrollment of mobile devices. It also enrolls Mac computers. It is also used to provision AMT-based computers.

You can find the full list of site system roles at the following link:

http://technet.microsoft.com/en-us/library/gg712282.aspx

Site administration

Site administration activities include planning, analysis, installation, management, and monitoring of the System Center Configuration Manager 2012 R2 site hierarchy. There are three scenarios with respect to site hierarchy, and they are as follows:

- A standalone primary site.

- A primary site with one or more secondary sites.

- A central administration site with one or more primary sites. Each primary site in this configuration can have one or more secondary sites.

Different configurations apply to different parts in the site hierarchy. This means that some site system roles are only available in the central administration site and some are only available at a child primary or a standalone site. When you have a single standalone primary site, you have all of the site system roles at your disposal.

Planning and deploying sites

Deploying your first site defines the entire structure of your hierarchy. This primary site supports secondary sites, and it can be extended with a central administration site. You can get more information on how to extend a primary site with a central administration site at the following link:

`http://technet.microsoft.com/en-us/library/jj591551.aspx`

Deploying the central administration site as the first site will provide the flexibility to expand the hierarchy as your business needs and company grow.

More information about planning and deploying sites and defining the site hierarchy can be found at the following link:

`http://technet.microsoft.com/en-us/library/gg712681.aspx`

If you plan to use certificates in your System Center Configuration Manager hierarchy, you need to plan the dependencies for PKI in your infrastructure. You can read more about PKI certificate requirements for System Center Configuration Manager at the following link:

`http://technet.microsoft.com/en-us/library/gg699362.aspx`

For each site that you install, you have to install and configure site system roles for management. You have to review all the site system roles and see how to deploy them. For example, some roles require only one instance in the hierarchy and some roles require instances in each site. Finally, there are site system roles that can have multiple instances within a site.

If you deploy a central administration site, you can deploy site system roles that are used to monitor the entire hierarchy or roles that provide services for the entire hierarchy, such as the Endpoint Protection point. For primary sites, you need system roles for client communication, such as the software update point and the management point.

In order to plan your Configuration Manager's infrastructure better and deploy the site system roles in the most appropriate places, read the instructions at the following link:

```
http://technet.microsoft.com/en-us/library/gg712282.aspx#Plan_Where_
to_Install_Sites
```

After you deploy the first site, you can start configuring settings for hierarchy-wide operations and settings that are site-specific. Both configurations affect how sites operate and how clients function. The following is a list of some of the hierarchy-specific configurations:

- **Role-based authentication**: You can create administrative users who manage System Center Configuration Manager and give them specific roles and scopes.

- **Resource discovery**: You can discover active directory forests, groups, systems, users, network discovery, and heartbeat discovery.

- **Boundaries and boundary groups**: These groups control client site assignment and site system servers from which clients obtain an application and other content.

- **Client settings**: These settings specify how System Center Configuration Manager clients perform different tasks on the client machine. These tasks can check for new applications, check the hardware and software inventory, and so on.

Here are some site-specific settings:

- The summarization of status messages collected from the clients
- Maintenance tasks
- Site components that control how site system roles work in a site

Monitoring and maintaining the hierarchy

Monitoring and maintaining the status of the hierarchy is very important. The status can change over time and changes need to be addressed. To keep all the systems in prime condition, you must monitor the hierarchy for problems and take actions in order to prevent problems.

You can perform the monitoring tasks for the hierarchy by using the **Monitoring** section in the System Center Configuration Manager console and also configure maintenance tasks at each site to help maintain efficiency. System Center Configuration Manager provides built-in tasks that can be used to monitor and maintain the following:

- Reports that inform about the failure of tasks and operational status
- Receive alerts for current or upcoming problems
- Client statuses, which can show which clients are active
- View status of endpoint protection clients

Summary

This chapter was all about the initial setup of Configuration Manager 2012 R2. It showed you how to install and set up all of the prerequisites and requirements. After that, it explained the benefits of using Windows Server Failover Cluster on a database level and how to set up the database on a single server or on a Windows Server Failover Cluster. Then, the entire process of System Center Configuration Manager 2012 R2 installation was explained. In the end, there was an explanation on System Center Configuration Manager sites and site hierarchy as well as of the site features and functionalities.

In the next chapter, we will take a look at the Assets and Compliance section of System Center Configuration Manager 2012 R2 and learn how to configure it and use its functionalities, such as compliance management and configuring Endpoint Protection.

2
Assets and Compliance

The Asset Intelligence section of System Center Configuration Manager 2012 R2 gives you the ability to build inventories of your software licenses and also lets you manage them. It gives you an overview of the software installed on your infrastructure by keeping an Asset Intelligence catalog. Asset Intelligence uses **Windows Management Instrumentation (WMI)** to extract more detailed information from the hardware and software that is being used. SCCM 2012 R2 gives the users more than 60 different reports about the gathered asset information and displays them in a format that is easy to read. Most reports lead to more specific reports, where you can create custom queries to get detailed information. You can add custom information, such as custom software categories, software families, software labels, and hardware requirements, to the Asset Intelligence catalog.

SCCM 2012 R2 delivers an integrated, intelligent, and comprehensive overview of your company's software installations. It helps reduce the total cost of ownership of your application management life cycle, making software inventories by scanning all the hardware resources and translating inventoried data into useful information. You can limit software license usage by importing software license information into the Configuration Manager site's database. Asset Intelligence is very useful for keeping track of all the assets in your infrastructure, including software and hardware. The Asset Intelligence functionality in SCCM 2012 R2 can be used to inventory and report software that is in use in your infrastructure.

The benefits of centralized system management

System Center Configuration Manager 2012 R2 provides various means to manage and deliver different types of user experience, which might be based on identity, connectivity, and types of devices, all of this without having to give up control over protecting your assets. The following are the benefits of implementing System Center Configuration Manager 2012 R2:

- Workstation management: Online System Center offers a solution to the challenge of consumerization by enabling the management and monitoring of workstations and mobile devices, irrespective of whether they belong to the employer or the employee, regardless of their location. Device management is based on Microsoft System Center 2012 Configuration Manager using clients that can be installed from the management portal. Management features include asset inventory, software distribution, patch management, and deployment of images. In addition to these, Online System Center offers a comprehensive software packaging service with an option to automatize workstation preinstallations. You can read more about Online System Center at http://www.onlinesystemcenter.com.

- Mobile device management: Mobile device management enables the management of diverse mobile operating systems and smartphones, irrespective of whether they belong to the employer or the employee and the location. You can see all the included functions for mobile device management at http://technet.microsoft.com/en-us/library/dn376523.aspx#bkmk_comps.

- Enables users to be productive from anywhere on any device: This is done through a mechanism to manage a wide range of mobile devices using a single administration console. The product provides optimized and personalized application delivery, based on user identity, device type, and network capabilities. It also allows users to self-provision the application with the help of an online web-based application catalog. To use this function, you require a Windows Intune subscription.

- A unified management of the infrastructure, integrating client management functionalities and protecting against threats: Configuration Manager provides a single tool to manage all your client environments. It consolidates inventory management, software delivery, vulnerability prevention and remediation, and compliance reporting with a single infrastructure. It also offers remote controls, metering, operating system deployment, and so on.
- Simplified administration

In addition, System Center Configuration Manager 2012 R2 continues to get more integrated and comes with a common look and feel between the consoles of the various components. Combined with data integration between those components, both operationally and in a consolidated data warehouse, it gets more intertwined with cloud computing.

Managing compliance

Compliance settings provide you with the ability to define, monitor, enforce, and report a configuration's compliance. Compliance settings can handle the following scenarios, which all IT organizations have to deal with:

- Regulatory compliance: Regulatory compliance is a key scenario in many IT organizations. Regulatory compliance requires IT organizations to specify the security and privacy policies for corporate and user data as well as for IT systems. The difficult part for IT is to enforce and report on the enforcement of the set standards. Some IT companies find it difficult to enforce these policies and rely on scripts and tools that provide results on demand.

- Change verification: This scenario is used to verify a system's configuration before and after the planned changes have occurred. It allows you to confirm whether you are applying the changes to the specified systems.

- Configuration drift: This scenario is very common and known to IT personnel, but most IT companies do not consider the configuration drift. The drift starts when a system goes into production; as soon as multiple IT administrators start to deploy applications, troubleshoot issues, and so on, the system begins its drift from the standard. Over time, this drift can become unpredictable and can cause technical issues.

- Time to resolution: Most problems in the IT world occur due to human errors. These problems become the problem ticket that administrators have to handle. Stopping human errors is impossible, but identifying the human error quickly so that it can be resolved is the key to reducing the impact of such errors.

These scenarios come one by one or in combination, and they place a great overhead on IT. There is a small reward when they are successfully handled because they do not impact the business demand directly, and that is why they are liked less by the IT administrators. Compliance management doesn't eliminate these scenarios, but it makes them more manageable.

System Center Configuration Manager 2012 R2 has many new features, such as the following:

- A unified compliance and settings management across servers, desktops, laptops, and mobile devices
- Simplified administrator experience
- Role-based administration
- Simplified baseline creation experience
- Deployment of baselines
- The user and device targeting of baselines
- Defines compliance **service-level agreements (SLAs)** for baseline deployments and alert generation
- Monitors the baseline deployment compliance status
- Updated reports to include remediation, conflicts, and error reporting
- An automatic remediation for registry values, Windows Management Instrumentation (WMI) values, and script-based compliance checks
- Configuration item revisioning
- The migration of the existing Configuration Manager 2007 baselines and compliance items (configuration items)

Configuring compliance settings

Compliance settings are very easy to configure, unlike some other Configuration Manager features. The only prerequisites are the Configuration Manager installation and the client setting configuration, which will be discussed later. The client does all the processing and returns results to the server. The only requirements on the client side are as follows:

- Clients must have the Configuration Manager 2012 R2 Client agent installed
- Clients must have the .NET framework 2.0 installed

To enable compliance settings, proceed with the following steps:

1. Go to the **Administration** section and select **client settings**. Here, you can edit the existing settings or create a new set of client settings.
2. To edit the existing set, right-click on it and select **properties**. If you want to create a new set of settings, select **Create Custom Client Device Settings**.
3. After the client settings are deployed, the client's compliance settings are enabled on the client. This is all that is required to configure Configuration Manager compliance management.

Configuration items and baselines

Compliance is configured by creating two object types:

- Configuration items: This is a set of settings and criteria that define what is compared, checked, and evaluated.
- Configuration baselines: This is a group of multiple configuration items. Configuration items must be part of a configuration baseline for them to be subjected to evaluation by a collection of systems.

There are many combinations of compliance settings because each organization is unique and requires a specific configuration of the system. Compliance settings give you the tools that help you create configuration items and baselines from scratch, according to your specific needs and wants. The following two topics explain the details of baselines and configuration items and the editor used to create and modify them.

Configuration items

Configuration items are used to encapsulate all the checks that compliance settings perform against the target system to determine its compliance. These checks are also called the evaluation criteria. To view or edit the configuration items on a particular site, click on the **Assets and Compliance** section of the Configuration Manager console and select **Compliance Settings**.

You can use search filters and saved searches to find specific configuration items, or you can just limit the results from the search that is displayed. Some of the most used search criteria are the following:

- **Revision**: This field shows the highest number of revisions of the configuration item
- **Child**: This field shows that a configuration item is a child item
- **Relationship**: This field shows that the configuration item is a parent of another configuration item
- **Categories**: This field shows the categories that the item belongs to
- **Device type**: This can be either a Windows configuration item or a mobile configuration item

In addition, there are four configuration item types:

- **Applications**: This configuration item checks whether an application exists on a target machine and checks the corresponding settings.
- **Software updates**: This configuration update checks the patch and update levels of a target system. The evaluation criteria are the installation statuses of the patch or the update. To use this configuration item, you first need to configure the Configuration Manager Software Update feature.
- **Operating system**: This configuration item looks for a specific operating system's version and settings. The version is selected from a preconfigured drop-down list.
- **General**: This configuration item is used for mobile devices.

In order to create a new configuration item, you have to select **Create Configuration Item** from the ribbon at the top or right-click on the context menu. This will start a wizard that will guide you through the rest of the process. The following are the steps that you need to perform for all the options:

- **General**: In this page, specify the name of the configuration item and its description. The choice you make determines which pages will be shown.

- **Configuration item**: In addition, you have to select the type of configuration item that you want to create:

    ○ **Windows**: This is applied only to Windows systems.

    ○ **Mobile device**: This is applied to fully supported mobile devices, but it does not include devices managed by the Exchange ActiveSync Connector. To see the full list of supported devices, go to `http://technet.microsoft.com/en-us/library/gg682077.aspx`.

- **Detection methods**: This page is only for Windows configuration items and is only shown if the **This configuration item contains application settings** checkbox is checked in the general tab. Here, you specify the criteria for application detection. There are three ways to do this:

    ○ **Always assume that the application is installed**: This means that the client always assumes that the application is installed.

    ○ **Use Windows installer detection**: This setting uses the Windows installer list of products to determine whether the application exists on the target system. If the application is not installed with MSI, then this method cannot be applied. You can also use WMI to determine the application's version and GUID. Here is the command-line syntax to do that:

    ```
    wmic product where "caption like '%Live%'" get name,
    IdentifyingNumber, version
    ```

    ○ **Custom scripts**: This method uses a custom script (VBScript, Jscript, or PowerShell-based) to detect the installation of an application. The script should return some text to indicate the successful detection of an installed application and should not return text to indicate failure. A simple example of VBScript to detect the installation of the Internet Explorer Administration Kit 7 is given as follows:

    ```
    folderPath = "C:\Program Files\Microsoft IEAK 7"
    Set fso = CreateObject("Scripting.FileSystemObject")
    If fso.FolderExists(folderPath) Then
    WScript.Echo "IEAK 7 Found"
    End If
    ```

- **Settings**: In this page, you can configure the settings that the client will evaluate. You can specify the following:
  - ○ Name
  - ○ Description
  - ○ Setting type
  - ○ Data type

- **Compliance rules**: These rules determine how the client will evaluate each setting in a configuration item. Without compliance rules, settings are meaningless.

- **Supported platforms**: In this page, you can select the platforms that this configuration item applies. All the supported versions of Windows and all mobile device platforms are listed. If the client platform is not listed, the configuration item is not evaluated.

- **Mobile device settings**: Here, you specify a group of settings that the client will evaluate on the target mobile device system. Each selected group will add new pages to the wizard.

- **Platform applicability**: This page shows all the mobile device settings chosen and configured on the mobile device settings page.

- **Summary**: This is a list of all the choices you made in the wizard.

- **Progress**: This shows the progress in creating the configuration item.

- **Completion**: This is the results page that lists the errors that occurred and the warnings that were given during the item creation process.

Configuration baselines

Configuration baselines are groups of configuration items. Configuration baselines are always deployed to collections that need evaluation. You can add any number of items to a baseline. Also, you can add a baseline in a baseline. The result is a group of settings of the configuration items it contains. To start configuring baselines, go to the **Compliance Settings** menu in the **Assets and Compliance** section of the Configuration Manager console and select **Baselines**. You can limit the displayed baselines using the following search filters:

- **Revision**: This shows the highest number of revisions of the configuration baseline

- **Compliance count**: This shows the number of systems that comply with the baseline

- **Noncompliance count**: This shows the number of systems that do not comply with the baseline

- **Failure count**: This shows the number of systems that encountered an error during evaluation

- **Categories**: This shows the defined categories for the configuration baseline

To create a new baseline, you have to select **Create Configuration Baseline** from the ribbon bar or right-click on the context menu. On the first page, specify the name and description of the baseline. In the bottom of the page, select all the categories that this baseline will belong to. Categories don't have any function out of the Configuration Manager console.

The main activity in baseline creation is to select the configuration data that it will contain. This can be done using the **Add** button from the configuration data listbox. Three options are available:

- **Configuration items**
- **Software updates**
- **Configuration baselines**

Application configuration items can have one of the following purposes:

- **Requires**: The application defined in the configuration item must exist on the target system

- **Optional**: Settings are evaluated only if the application exists on the target system

- **Prohibited**: The application in the configuration item must now exist on the target system

Software updates are always set as required, and they must always exist on the target system. Like software updates, baselines are also set as required, but this means nothing because the important aspect here is the evaluation condition of the configuration items it contains. To modify a baseline, select the baseline and choose **Properties** from the ribbon or right click on the context menu. You can also disable a baseline from the ribbon or by right-clicking on the context menu.

Baseline deployment

Baselines are deployed on a set of target client systems defined by a collection. Each baseline has a different evaluation schedule defined in the default client settings for the hierarchy. To deploy a baseline, select the configuration baselines node or any other configuration baseline and choose **Deploy** from the ribbon bar or right-click on the context menu. This opens up the **Deploy Baseline** dialog, which contains the following information:

- Included configuration baselines
- Remediation for noncompliant rules
- Console alert generation
- System Center Operations Manager alerts
- Target collection
- The baseline evaluation schedule

You can deploy baselines to either user or device collections. If a baseline contains user evaluation criteria, only these criteria will be evaluated. This means that when you deploy a baseline make sure that you have at least one valuation criteria for a user or a device.

System Center Configuration Manager keeps track of all the baseline deployments. To view all the deployments for a baseline, select the baseline; at the bottom, you will see a details pane. This pane has a **Deployment** tab. If you select this tab, you will see all the deployments for the selected baseline. In order to examine or modify a deployment, you can go to the **Monitoring** section of the Configuration Manager console and click on the **Deployments** node. You will find all the deployments here, not just the baseline deployments. There is a console search and filtering functionality that you can use to find deployments that you want to view or modify. One thing that needs to be mentioned here is that you cannot delete a deployment from the **Monitoring** section. You must delete the baseline from the **Assets and Compliance** section. To modify a deployment, select it and choose **Properties** from the ribbon bar or right-click on the context menu.

Compliance evaluation

Clients receive compliance baseline deployments from the Management Point, which is set in the client policy. The information needed for configuration settings' compliance scans often takes more than one client-policy refresh cycle to be staged on the client side. During this, the status of the scan will not match the expectations.

According to baseline deployment, clients evaluate configuration items from the baseline using compliance rules and evaluation schedules. The evaluation usually starts a couple of hours after the start defined in the schedule. There are four different compliance states for a baseline deployment:

- **Compliant**: This means that the target system is in line with the compliance rules in the baseline evaluation conditions
- **Error**: This means that an error occurred on the client system while evaluating the baseline
- **Noncompliant**: This means that the target system is not in line with the compliance rules in the baseline evaluation condition
- **Unknown**: This means that the target system has not reported its status for the baseline

When a compliance rule fails, the configuration item, as a whole, is marked as noncompliant and one of the following noncompliance messages is reported:

- None
- Information
- Warning
- Critical
- Critical with an event

Compliance rules that fail with the critical event's noncompliant message add an entry to the Windows application event log. Based on these entries, you can configure actions in the scheduled tasks or you can use System Center Operations Manager to generate alerts. Baseline and configuration item evaluations are client-side tasks. Results are sent to the site using the state message mechanism inside the Configuration Manager. You can read more about this mechanism at the following blog:

```
http://blogs.msdn.com/b/steverac/archive/2011/01/07/sccm-state-
messaging-in-depth.aspx
```

Configuration Manager clients keep a baseline evaluation cache of 15 minutes. The client will not evaluate the baseline until this 15-minute interval expires, unless the baseline deployment has changed. Even if it is configured for a shorter evaluation period or for a manual trigger, the evaluation using System Center Configuration Manager control panel applet.

Configuration packs

System Center Configuration Manager has a large number of predefined configuration baselines that can be used as a starting point. This is because the requirements between different IT organizations are similar. They are contained in a configuration pack, which is analogous to a management pack in System Center Operations Manager. Configuration packs such as management packs can be downloaded for free from the following link:

`http://systemcenter.pinpoint.microsoft.com/en-US/home`.

The types of configuration packs available for download are:

- **Regulatory compliance**: These configuration packs are for regulatory compliance, such as SOX, HIPAA, or EUDPD.

- **Best practices**: These configuration packs are made from the best practices followed by Microsoft's internal IT departments.

- **Third-party software and hardware**: Similar to the management packs in System Center Operations Manager, which include many packs developed for third-party software and hardware, there are configuration packs designed and developed for configuration enforcement for third-party application software.

There are many configuration packs for Configuration Manager 2007 that are compatible with System Center Configuration Manager 2012 R2. When you download the configuration pack, the next thing you have to do is to install it. To do this, you have to perform the following steps:

1. Open the **Assets and Compliance** section from the console.

2. Select configuration items or configuration baselines and then select **Import Configuration Data** from the ribbon or right-click on the context menu.

3. This will start the import configuration wizard, and on the **Select Files** page, click on the **Add** button to browse the CAB file of the configuration pack. You can also import multiple CAB files.

4. Click on **Next** to proceed to the **Summary** page, where you can go through the configuration items and baselines included in the configuration pack that is being imported.

5. Complete the wizard.

Exporting configuration items and baselines

Exporting configuration items and baselines gives you the ability to share them with a different Configuration Manager site; you can edit them or view them in a native XML format.

The export created a CAB file in a specified folder during the export. The CAB file is an XML file, so if you are familiar with it you can edit the XML file. The XML file can also be viewed from the console by clicking on **View xml definition**.

Compliance authoring

Configuration Manager is responsible for creating, organizing, editing, and deploying compliance settings. The biggest challenge is when you have to translate business requirements into Configuration Manager items.

Organization

The organization of configuration items in configuration baselines is very important, just as in the case of organizing individual policies within Group Policy Objects. Actually, you don't need any organization. If you put all the settings in one configuration item and baseline, you are done. However, the problem is when something goes wrong and you have to troubleshoot an issue. Organize similar settings into a single configuration item; for example, put all the settings for Internet Explorer into one configuration item. For more isolation, you can create a baseline with just one configuration item.

Although this is a good practice and creates isolation, it creates a lot of configuration items and more overhead for administration. Think of the configuration items as building blocks representing atomic units of functionality. Combining these in different ways results in a diverse and comprehensive set of baselines that are easier to maintain and troubleshoot.

Evaluation is mostly quick and has no major impact on the client system. However, it is possible to create complex configuration items or baselines with a lot of configuration settings, but this will affect the target system. Software updates' compliance terms have a great impact on the client performance, especially when many are packed in one baseline. Test the baseline before deploying it so that you ensure that it won't affect performance on the target system. Scripts also have a great impact on target systems and because of this Configuration Manager 2012 R2 has a 1-minute timeout for scripts.

Using Microsoft tools

A great way to start configuring compliance settings is with the help of Microsoft configuration packs. They provide great examples and are good to use as a reference because they can teach you about compliance settings. Many of the evaluation checks are performed by custom scripts, and you can use them in your own configuration settings as well as easily modify them.

Security Compliance Manager

Security Compliance Manager is a Microsoft tool that is free for download. You can download it from the following link:

```
http://www.microsoft.com/download/en/details.
aspx?displaylang=en&id=16776
```

This tool can help you to create and manage configuration baselines. The difference is that it cannot apply baselines to target systems and that is why it relies on Configuration Manager and group policies to do that. This tool includes a lot of baselines that cover the Windows, Microsoft Office, and Internet Explorer configurations. SCM has the capability to import a Group Policy Object, and this is a great way to start your baseline creation. When you have defined your baseline configuration, you can export it and import the Configuration Manager compliance settings.

CP Studio

This is a third-party application from Silect Software (`http://www.silect.com`). It is similar to SCM because it offers the authoring of configuration baselines and configuration items. This allows IT administrators to create baselines without the Configuration Manager console. CP Studio provides a rich and intuitive environment for baseline creation. This is important because it shortens the development life cycle of configuration baselines and decreases the time needed for baselines to be put into production.

The compliance strategy

All of the functionalities regarding compliance settings are relatively straightforward. You have to create the settings and deploy them. However, the main thing is what should be done after that. Configuration manager clients will accumulate data, and you have to decide what is to be done with this data. Some of the goals might be satisfying business goals, creating reports, troubleshooting, correcting nonstandard configurations, and so on. Every baseline that you create can address some of these goals. So, that is why the first thing to do is to identify the baseline's purpose, target, and delivery method. The following three parameters define what you put inside a baseline:

- **Reporting**: This consists of another way to view and distribute the compliance results of the deployed baselines.

- **Alerting**: This consists of raising real-time alerts of the evaluation results of a baseline.

- **On-demand results**: This deals with client-side report generation. You can trigger the evaluation on the clients of selected baselines.

Endpoint Protection

Configuration Manager 2007 provided Endpoint Protection as an add-on. In the newest release of Configuration Manager 2012 and 2012 R2, this is a built-in feature. Endpoint Protection allows IT administrators to monitor and control the security state of the client workstations from one console and perform easy administration tasks.

Integrating client management and client security in one console cuts down costs. IT administrators now focus on end-to-end security tasks and manage, report, and react to issues with clients from a common console. The best features of Endpoint Protection are as follows:

- **Licensing**: To implement Endpoint Protection, you need to have a license to use it. The license is called Core Client Access License or CAL.

- **Customizable**: You can create custom client settings and target different device collections. You can find preconfigured malware policies to speed up the deployment process.

- **Separate client**: Endpoint Protection uses a different client from the one that the Configuration Manager uses. The functionalities of the System Center Endpoint Protection client are:

    - Easy to deploy
    - Autouninstallation of third-party software
    - Malware and spyware detection and remediation
    - Rootkit detection and remediation
    - Vulnerability assessment and automatic definition updates
    - Integrated with the Windows firewall
    - Network vulnerability detection using a network inspection system

In System Center Configuration Manager 2012 and 2012 R2, in order to configure Endpoint Protection, you need to enable the site system role. You do not have to run a separate installer, and you also don't need a different console. You can go to the **Monitoring** section and see the **Endpoint Protection** menu. The administration of Endpoint Protection is very simple because it is role-based. You can create security roles and assign them to specific users from your company. System Center Endpoint Protection, on a target client machine, is installed together with the Configuration Manager client. If no other malware policy exists, the default malware policy is included in it. This happens when System Center Endpoint Protection is enabled in the default client settings. Endpoint Protection uses the same database as the Configuration Manager, so you do not need to install a separate database. Endpoint Protection uses real-time e-mail notifications.

Prerequisites for Endpoint Protection

Before installing Endpoint Protection, you have to fulfill these prerequisites:

- Windows Server Update Services are required if you are using the Configuration Manager software update point role to deliver antimalware definition updates.

- If you want to deploy firewall policies to Windows Server 2008 or Windows Vista SP1, you must install this hotfix:

  http://support.microsoft.com/kb/971800

- One of the options for client computers to synchronize antimalware definition updates is to have Internet access.

- The Endpoint Protection site system role must be running on your central administration site or on a primary site and on a site system server only.

- A software update point must be installed and configured in order to deliver definitions and updates.

- You must install reporting services and the reporting services point to display Endpoint Protection reports.

- Security permissions must be defined to manage Endpoint Protection. There is a built-in security role called Endpoint Protection Manager; this grants permissions to define and monitor security policies.

Planning for Endpoint Protection

Enabling Endpoint Protection point site system role is very easy, but you should carefully plan how you will deploy agents in your hierarchy. It is strongly recommended that you don't use the default client settings, as this will propagate them to all the clients.

Creating client settings and antimalware policies

A best practice is to create custom client settings for Endpoint Protection and to deploy them to a collection that is created only for Endpoint Protection. You can create many custom client settings for Endpoint Protection to target computers with settings suited for function and purpose. Also, a good practice is to create different policies for servers and clients because you want to configure them in a way such that you can ignore or bypass certain Windows processes, processors, and disk load that would degrade the server's performance. You should create different antimalware policies for the different server platforms they target. Microsoft also provides server-specific antimalware policies that you can import and customize according to your needs. A good example of one of these policies is the built-in policy for Configuration Manager 2012, which is `SCEP12_Default_ConfigMgr2012.xml`. This policy combines the default server's workload policy settings with settings that are optimized for System Center 2012 Configuration Manager, in particular the settings for file and folder exclusions. The logic here is that server-specific roles do certain things repeatedly and consistently, and you want your antimalware solution to exclude certain processes and files that are regularly used by that specific server role.

A failure to add these exclusions can affect the server performance and cause additional issues, such as loss of communication and network issues.

Deploying to a test collection

Prior to the initial setup of Endpoint Protection in your hierarchy, you should always deploy the agent to a test collection in order to test the settings. This will verify that your custom client settings and antimalware policies function properly on the target system. A definition or an engine update can cause problems on the client computer. Usually, these problems manifest with a blue screen of death or some hardware scenarios. Some updates even block files that might be vital to the business. When you face this kind of a scenario, you can deploy a script through packages/programs. The script should run the following code:

```
mpcmdrun.exe -removedefinitions [All]
```

This will remove any updates and will revert to the previous definition. Also, make sure that you prevent the client from installing the updates again. Endpoint Protection in System Center Configuration Manager 2012 does not contain any of the collections that Manager 2007 came with. Those collections were used to sort computers with malware-related issues into predefined locked-query based collections. You could not edit or view the queries in such collections; however, third parties later released the contents of these queries online in an Excel format, just in case you want to recreate the collections. You don't have to create these collections in System Center 2012 Endpoint Protection; the Endpoint Protection status dashboard replaces this functionality by letting you see the malware and operational state of the entire selected collection. These items are clickable, allowing the administrator to drill down into reports or take recommended actions. Here are the malware remediation status items that are viewable in the dashboard:

- Remediation failed
- Full scan required
- Restart required
- Offline scan required
- Client settings modified by malware
- Malware remediated in the last 24 hours

In addition to the functionality in the dashboard, you can easily build collections based on the new Endpoint Protection classes; these are the same classes as the ones used in the predefined FEP 2010 collections, making those collections unnecessary as you can easily build your own. You have to create separate custom client and antimalware policies and then target device collections. To do this, you can create folders specific to Endpoint Protection, such as:

- Endpoint Protection managed client computers
- Endpoint Protection managed server

After this, you can put a device collection into these folders and target them with different custom client settings and antimalware policies. Servers are critical to the organization, so you should create multiple server device collections to separate different server roles. This is a best practice because SQL Server should be treated differently than Hyper-V hosts or other types of servers, for example, a Web server.

The suggested device collection name for Windows client computers is Endpoint Protection Managed Desktop and Laptops, which can be created in the Endpoint Protection managed client computers' folder that we talked about earlier. Use these device collections only for Endpoint Protection, and create other device collections for other deployments. Here is a list of the suggested collections:

- Endpoint Protection Managed Servers – Domain Controller
- Endpoint Protection Managed Servers – Exchange
- Endpoint Protection Managed Servers – Operations Manager
- Endpoint Protection Managed Servers – Configuration Manager
- Endpoint Protection Managed Servers – SQL 2008
- Endpoint Protection Managed Servers – File Server
- Endpoint Protection Managed Servers – Service Manager
- Endpoint Protection Managed Servers – Data Protection Manager
- Endpoint Protection Managed Servers – IIS Web Server
- Endpoint Protection Managed Servers – Hyper-V
- Endpoint Protection Managed Servers – Terminal Server
- Endpoint Protection Managed Servers – Other Servers

You should place all of the device collections in the Endpoint Protection Managed Servers folder and target them with antimalware policies that best suit them. The key point here is to target specific server roles with customized antimalware rule sets configured to allow optimum performance and availability, even when they are protected via Endpoint Protection. The SCEP client can handle servers in multiple device collections targeted by multiple antimalware policies; however, the policy with the highest priority takes precedence. You can also mix policies for different server roles and combine them into one.

Installing the Endpoint Protection role

Prior to installing the Endpoint Protection role, you must determine its place in the Configuration Manager hierarchy. If you have multiple sites in your hierarchy, you have to install the role on top of these sites in your Central Administration site. If you have a standalone primary site, you have to install the role on it. The Endpoint Protection role can be installed only on one site system server in the Configuration Manager hierarchy. When you enable the Endpoint Protection role, the following actions are performed:

- You are presented with the EULA or the end user's license agreement
- The default Microsoft active protection service configuration is set
- The System Center Endpoint Protection client is installed on the server hosting the role

When you enable the Endpoint Protection role, the Endpoint Protection client is installed on the machine hosting this role. This client is used to download and host the definition file. The server then pools this client and gets the malware data into the database. The client doesn't have scans and services enabled, so it can run together with other antimalware solutions on the server. The following example is for a hierarchy containing multiple sites:

1. Go to the **Administration** section. In the navigation tree on the left-hand side, select **Overview** and expand **Site Configuration**. Then, select **Servers and Site System Roles**. Here, you will be able to see all the installed site systems:

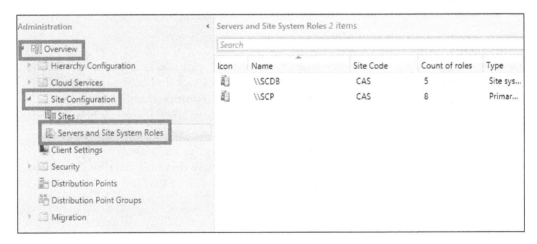

2. Select the CAS site server or the standalone primary server and right-click on it. Select **Add Site System Roles**.

3. When you reach the system role page of the add site system role wizard or create site system server wizard, select **Endpoint Protection point**. The wizard looks for the Software Update Point role. If it is not installed, you need to install it. If you choose to go through without the software update point, then you have to adjust the default antimalware policy to prevent it from retrieving updates from Configuration Manager:

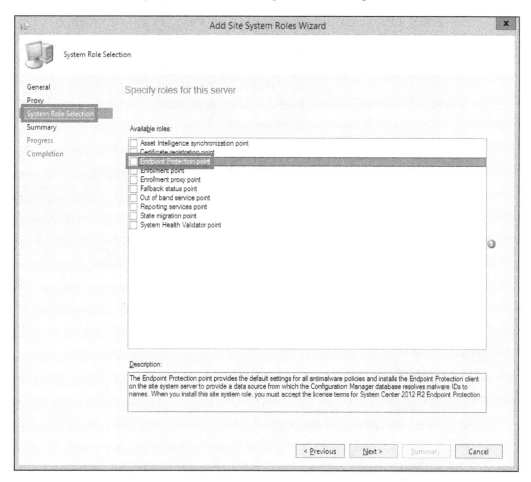

4. On the Endpoint Protection page, you must accept the license terms and continue with the wizard.

5. On the Microsoft active protection service page, you can choose from the following three options available:

   ○ **I do not want to join Microsoft active protection service**

   ○ **Basic membership**

   ○ **Advanced membership**

Microsoft active protection service or MAPS, formerly known as SpyNet, allows you to send information to Microsoft about the software you detect. This data is used for the creation of new definitions that improve the security and protection levels of your infrastructure. The second option allows you to join the information exchange. With advanced membership, MAPS sends more detailed information about the detected software and alerts the user. A best practice is to choose basic membership because it provides you with a higher level of security.

6. Go through the remaining steps of the wizard. You can change MAPS's membership settings if you go to the **Administration** section and navigate to **Overview | Site Configuration | Server and Site Systems**. Select the site server from the list, right click on the Endpoint Protection point, and select **Properties** in the details pane at the bottom. You can verify the successful installation of the Endpoint Protection role by taking a look at the `EPsetup.log` file contained in the server's logfile directory for any errors. Here, you should see lines similar to the following:

```
SMSEP Setup Started....
Installing the SMSEP
Unable to query registry key
(SOFTWARE\Microsoft\Windows\CurrentVersion\Uninstall\Microsoft
Security Client),
return (0x00000002) means EP client is NOT installed
Installation was successful.
```

Setting up a software update point for Endpoint Protection

If you want to use the software update point role to synchronize and use software updates in order to automatically download and deploy definition updates to your Endpoint Protection client, you must configure it properly. It allows you to synchronize with the Microsoft Windows update on a predefined schedule in order to enable protection for your client machines. It downloads the latest antimalware and engine updates in an automated way. After the download, the updates need to be deployed. This can be done by creating automatic deployment rules. This is an optional way of doing it; you can also perform the tasks manually.

Configuring the SUP to synchronize definition updates

In order to deliver the Endpoint Protection engine and definition updates from the software update point, you must ensure that it is configured to synchronize **Definition Updates**, as shown in the following screenshot:

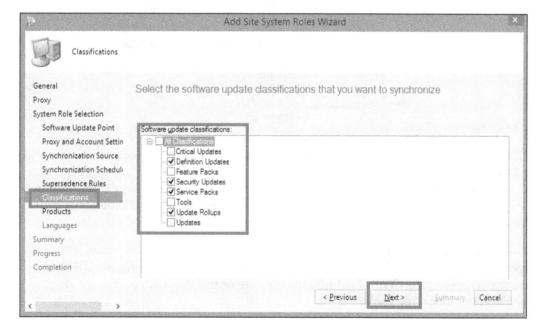

Here, you can configure which updates will be synchronized by the SUP. Also, select the **Forefront Endpoint Protection 2010** product, which is listed in the **Products** tab, as shown in the following screenshot:

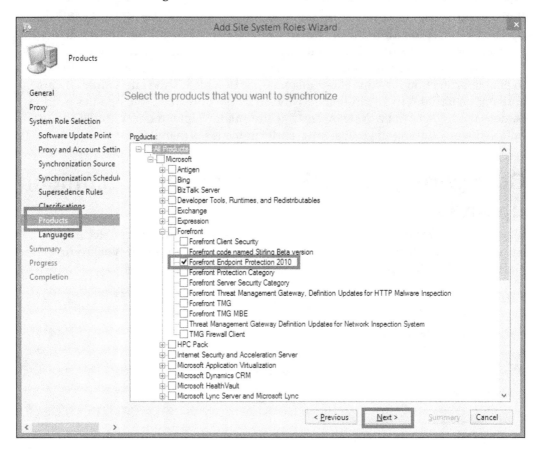

Don't get confused by the version mismatch between System Center Configuration Manager 2012 and Endpoint Protection 2010 because the Endpoint Protection 2010 Version is included in the Configuration Manager 2012 Version.

Endpoint Protection definition updates are released several times per day, so you should configure them for download at least once per day. To configure SUP with these changes on the Central Administration site or the standalone primary site, perform the following steps:

1. Go to the **Administration** workspace.

2. Navigate to **Overview | Site Configuration | Sites** and from the list, select **CAS**. Click on **Settings** in the ribbon bar. Select **configure site components** from the drop-down menu and click on **software update point**.

3. Select the **Classification** tab, check **Definition Updates,** and click on **Apply**.

4. Select the **Products** tab and check **Forefront Endpoint Protection 2010** from the list.

5. Select the **Sync Schedule** tab and adjust the schedule to **Simple Schedule for every 1 days**. To set the actual time, go to **Custom Schedule**.

6. Click on **OK** to initiate the synchronization as soon as possible.

Creating autodeployment rules for definition updates

The software update point is used for the new autodeployment rules feature. This eliminates the need to approve updates in WSUS. They can also be easily scaled. This feature gives instructions to automatically download and deploy specific software updates on a predefined schedule. To configure **Automatic Deploy Rules (ADR)** for Endpoint Protection, perform the following steps:

1. Go to the **Software Library** workspace.

2. Select **Software Updates** and expand all the software updates. Right click on it and choose **Run Synchronization**. You can verify that the synchronization is complete at the site by the following methods:

   ° Review **Software Update Point Synchronization Status** in the **Monitoring** workspace. Verify that the synchronization status is completed.

   ° Review SMS_WSUS_SYNC_MANAGER and look for the message ID 6702, WSUS. Verify that the synchronization status is completed.

   ° Review the WSUSsyncmgr.log file and look for **Sync Succeeded**.

3. Expand **Software Updates** and select **Automatic Deployment Rules**.

4. In the ribbon bar, click on **Create Automatic Deployment Rule**. This starts the automatic deployment rule wizard.

Here, you can give the rule a name, such as `ADR: Endpoint protection managed client computers`, and point it to a collection you want to target. As you will update this collection regularly, select **Add to an existing Software Update Group**, as shown in the following screenshot:

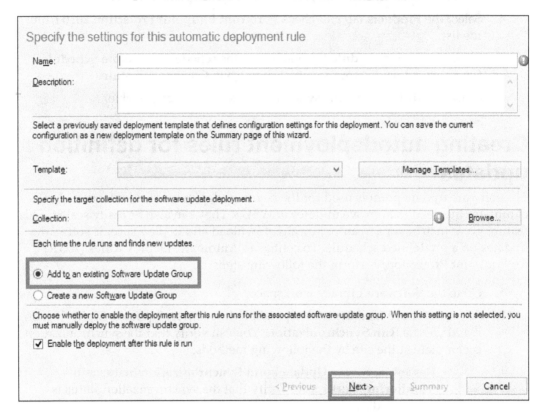

5. The **Deployment Settings** page of the wizard lets you select **Use Wake-on-LAN** to wake up the client machines for the required deployments. This is useful when you need to deploy updates during the night, when the client machines are turned off. Starting with Configuration Manager R2, you can define templates. These templates have preconfigured settings for **Definition Updates**:

   ○ On the **Software Updates** page, you can choose the parameters you want to check when ADR runs.

    ◦   In the **Evaluation Schedule** section, click on **Customize and set it run every 1 days**. Also, make sure that the ADR schedule does not exceed the SUP schedule because you will evaluate for new definitions and your SUP synchronizes once per day.

    ◦   In the **Deployment Schedule** screen, you can set the time based on UTC. This allows clients to install updates at the same time. This setting is a recommended best practice.

    ◦   On the **User Experience** page, you can hide the definition update notifications because they can occur frequently. Select **Hide** in the software center, and select all the notifications from the drop-down menu.

    ◦   On the **Alerts** page, you can enable options to generate alerts according to your SLA agreement.

    ◦   On the **Download Settings** page, you can specify the download settings for these definition updates.

On the **Deployment Package** page, there are two options:

> **Select deployment package**: You can use this option when you have a deployment package already created
>
> **Create a new definition package**: You can use this option when you want to create a new deployment package

6. Go through the rest of the wizard and review the summary. You can wait for the ADR to run automatically or you can run it manually. If it runs successfully, it will display **Last Error Description of Success and Last Error Code 0x00000000**. This can also be disabled and enabled at any time.

Working with antimalware policies

Antimalware policies define how the SCEP client is configured for key security behaviors, such as scheduled scans, scan settings, actions to be taken if malware is found, real-time protection, behavior monitoring, exclusion settings, where to get the definition updates from, and much more. These topics are discussed in the following sections.

Understanding the default antimalware policy

The default client antimalware policy is the policy applied to the client at initial installation. The settings that are contained in this policy are divided into sections. Each section has the following configurable options:

- **Scheduled scans**: This option allows you to specify whether to run scans on target computers or not. There are two options under this setting: full scan and quick scan. A full scan takes more time to complete because it scans everything and everywhere. You can set the day and time for the full scan setting. You can also configure the target computer to look for updates before the full scan and to perform the full scan only when the client is idle.

- **Scan settings**: Here, you can define whether you want to scan e-mails, attachments, archived files, or removable devices. You can also scan network drives, but make sure that they are on a fast network because the scan will take longer to finish.

- **Default actions**: In Endpoint Protection, four levels are defined for the malware: severe, high, medium, and low. When malware is detected, it is rated with one of these levels. When malware with a severe risk level is detected, you can set a default action to be applied.

- **Real-time protection**: This setting lets you scan files and processes in real time. To enable real-time protection, just set it to true in the default antimalware policy.

- **Exclusion settings**: These are very important because they let you mark folders that will not be part of the scanning process. These folders are used by a known application and processes that perform read and write operations in them so that you know that they are not suspicious and you can exclude them from the scan.

- **Advanced**: The advanced settings allow you to create a system restore point before the target computer is cleaned of the malware. You can set up notifications for the end users, when users need to perform certain actions.

- **Threat overrides**: Regarding threat overrides, there are three options: allow, remove, or quarantine. These actions are applied when certain types of malware or virus is detected.

- **Definition updates**: This setting defines how frequently the System Center Endpoint Protection agent will update definitions. You can set different update intervals for definition updates, such as in specific hours or at a specific time of the day. You can also set the source for the updates. It can be Configuration Manager, UNC file share, WSUS, Microsoft update, or Microsoft Malware Protection Center.

Creating a custom antimalware policy

In every section of the antimalware policy, you will find the statement *custom policies override the default policy*. This is a reminder that a best practice is to always create a custom policy and configure it according to your needs. After you create the policy, be sure to test it on some device collection containing computers.

Importing and merging antimalware policies

As mentioned earlier, there are several examples of antimalware policies provided by Microsoft. You can import them and combine them together to create a new policy. To import a policy, you have to do the following:

1. Go to the **Assets and Compliance** section. From the navigation tree, navigate to **Overview** | **Endpoint Protection** | **Antimalware Policies**.

2. From the ribbon bar, select **Import**.

3. Select the policy you want to import.

4. When the import is complete, the policy is opened for editing. When you finish editing, click on **OK**. The imported policy is now available and appears in the console.

Merging policies

Merging policies can be very useful. Consider a server that has several functions and that each of these functions has a different antimalware policy. If you merge all of these policies, you will get one policy for this kind of server. To merge policies, do the following:

1. Go to **Assets and Compliance** and from the navigation tree, expand **Overview**. Select **Endpoint Protection** and then click on **Antimalware Policies**.

2. Select all the policies you want to merge and click on **Merge** from the ribbon bar, as shown in the following screenshot:

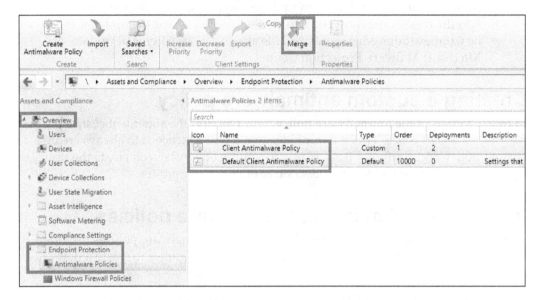

3. You will have to enter a new policy name.

4. You have to select a base policy. This is the policy from which the overall antimalware policy settings are taken and are merged with the exclusion of the other policies selected.

5. The merged policy appears in the console and is ready for deployment. The original policies also remain in the console.

Configuring alerts for Endpoint Protection

Alerts can be very useful when specific events occur in the hierarchy, and you can notify responsible users when malware is detected. Alerts are displayed in the **Monitoring** section under the alerts node. A best practice is to set up e-mail notifications because IT administrators might not always be in front of the Configuration Manager console. Most IT administrators have mobile phones that can send and receive e-mails directly from the phone. This is important because they can receive the e-mail in real time and respond accordingly.

Configuring e-mail notifications

In order to configure e-mail notifications, you must have an SMTP server in your infrastructure. In a multisite hierarchy, you only need to specify the e-mail server at the top, that is, the CAS. An e-mail notification by itself will not alert IT administrators if malware is detected. You also need to configure alert subscriptions to be notified by e-mail for specific alerts. Different e-mail addresses can be specified, and this is a recommended practice to receive e-mail notifications. By having more than one person receive the e-mail alerts, you have more chances to minimize the effects of the malware. To configure e-mail notifications, do the following:

1. Go to the **Administration** workspace.

2. Navigate to **Overview** | **Site Configuration** | **Sites**. Select **Settings** from the ribbon bar, click on **Configure Site Components**, and choose **Email Notification**:

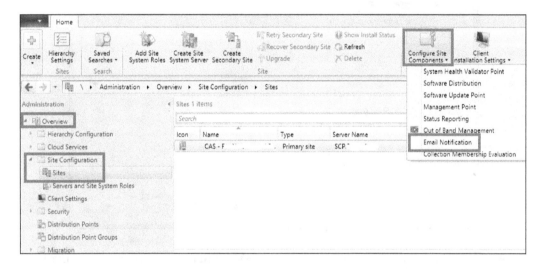

3. Enter the FQDN or the IP address of the SMTP server and specify the SMTP port. Select **None** if the server doesn't require authentication; if it requires authentication, enter an account to authenticate. You need to specify the sender address, which might not exist; however, if you want people to reply to it, you need a real e-mail address:

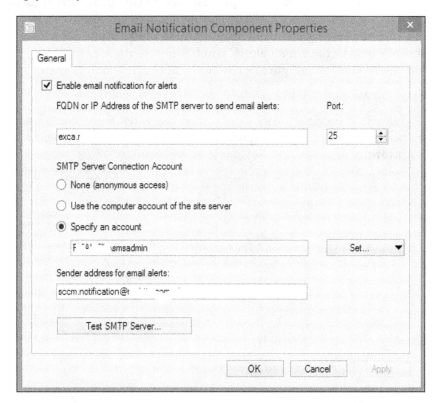

4. To test the SMTP server, click on **Test SMTP Server...**. Enter a test e-mail recipient address and click on **Send Test Email**. If everything is configured properly, the e-mail will reach the destination address and the message **Testing email was sent successfully please check your mailbox** will be displayed.

An e-mail notification alert consists of the following:

- The from address: This is the address that you specify in the sender address for e-mail alerts
- The subject of the e-mail, which consists of three pieces of information:
  - Description
  - Type of alert
  - Collection name
- Depending on the alert, the body of the e-mail will contain information about the breakout and might include information about the collection name, malware name, and successful remediation

Alert subscriptions

Alert subscriptions allow you to specify users who will receive e-mails when malware breakout occurs, but only if e-mail notifications are configured. For each subscription, you can specify multiple e-mail addresses. Each subscription can contain one or more criteria. To set up an alert subscription, do the following:

1. Go to the **Monitoring** section.
2. From the navigation tree, go to **Overview | Alerts | Subscriptions**.
3. From the ribbon bar, select **Create Subscription and Give it a Name**.
4. Select the e-mail language from the drop-down menu.
5. Choose **Alert** from the list. There are four types of alerts available:
   - Generate an alert when malware is detected
   - The same malware is detected on multiple computers
   - The same malware is detected repeatedly on a computer
   - Multiple types of malware are detected on a computer

   You need to select the type of alert and determine whether it is applicable to the device collection you want to monitor.

Configuring custom client device settings for Endpoint Protection

As a best practice, it is recommended that you create custom settings and not use the default settings. This is because default client settings apply to all the clients in the hierarchy. Any modification of the default settings will apply to all the clients. So, it is better to create custom client device settings for target device collections. Custom client settings always have a greater priority than the default client settings. To configure custom client device settings, do the following:

1. Go to the **Administration** section of the console.

2. In the navigation tree on the left, go to **Overview | Client Settings**.

3. Right click on it and select **Create Custom Client Device Settings**.

4. In the **Create Custom Client Device Settings** wizard, give the settings a name and select **Endpoint Protection** from the settings list.

5. Select **Endpoint Protection** on the left-hand side of the window, and on the right-hand side, configure the options as appropriate. A minimum configuration will include the first two options, which means that Endpoint Protection will manage the client computer and the System Center Endpoint Protection client will be installed.

6. Click on **OK** when you are done.

Deploying Endpoint Protection for custom client agent settings

After you finish configuring the custom client device settings, you have to deploy these settings and target device collections. Perform the following steps in order to deploy client settings to collections:

1. Go to the **Administration** workspace. From the navigation tree, go to **Overview | Client Settings**.

2. Right click on the previously created custom client device settings and select **Deploy**.

3. Select a device collection to which you will deploy the custom device settings and click on **OK**.

After this, any computer in the target device collection will receive the policy on the next policy update and the client will be installed. If the client is installed, it will not be reinstalled.

Monitoring the status of Endpoint Protection

The Endpoint Protection dashboard consists of three parts:

- **Collection**: This displays the object collection targeted by some antimalware client policy

- **Security state**: This shows the statistics of the Endpoint Protection client's status and displays information about the number of active protected clients and the number of active clients that are at risk

- **Operational state**: This shows the status of the malware definition update status on the clients

These sections give you information related to the last Endpoint Protection status on the currently selected collection. You can summarize this data if you click on **Run Summarization**, or you can schedule a recurring summarization if you click on **Schedule Summarization**. You can find both the options on the ribbon bar of the Configuration Manager console.

Configuring collections to appear in the collection view

To display information on the dashboard, you must configure collections to be viewed. To configure a collection to appear on the dashboard, go to the **Configuring Alerts for Device Collections** topic. When you finish configuring the collection, you can select it from the drop-down list. There are seven checkboxes provided:

- **Client check**
- **Client remediation**
- **Client activity**
- **Malware detection**
- **Malware outbreak**
- **Repeated malware detection**
- **Multiple malware detection**

Only malware alerts can be e-mailed, but all the seven checkboxes listed in the previous list can be viewed in the Endpoint Protection dashboard. To configure alerts for device collections, follow these steps:

1. Open the **Configuration Manager** console and go to the **Assets and Compliance** section.

2. From the navigation tree, go to **Overview | Device Collections** and select the **Endpoint Protection Managed Desktops and Laptops** collection.

3. Choose **Properties**, click on the **Alerts** tab, and check **View this collection in the Endpoint Protection Dashboard**.

4. Click on **Add** and select the multiple alerts you want to be notified for.

Security state view

This view gives you security information about the Endpoint Protection client's status and about any status regarding malware remediation. In the left-hand side pane, there are six clickable options:

- **Clients protected with endpoint protection**

  This option gives the number and percentage of clients from the device collection managed by Endpoint Protection that are not in a malware-pending remediation, don't have operation issues, and have up-to-date antivirus definitions.

- **At risk from malware or operational issue**

  This option gives a list of malware with pending remediation status, operational issues, and antivirus definitions that are older than one week.

- **Endpoint protection client not yet installed**

  This option shows the computers from the device collection that still haven't reported their statuses or don't have a SCEP client installed on them.

- **Endpoint protection client is not supported on the platform**

  This option shows the clients that have an OS that is not supported.

- **Configuration manager client inactive**

  This option lists whether Configuration Manager is inactive. This is defined in the activity settings. You can find them by navigating to **Monitoring | Overview | Client Status | Client Status Settings**.

- **Configuration manager client not installed**

  This option shows all the clients that do not have a SECP client installed on them.

Malware remediation status

When you go to the security area of the dashboard, in the right-hand side pane, there are several sections related to malware remediation. If a target system is found in a state that matches the items in this list, a link is added. This link leads to the **Assets and Compliance** section, and it gives you more details about the object. The items in the list are as follows:

- Remediation failed
- Full scan required
- Restart required
- Offline scan required
- Client settings modified by malware
- Malware remediated in the last 24 hours

Top malware

In the security area of the dashboard, in the bottom-right pane, there is information about the top malware by number of client computers in the last 24 hours. If no malware was found, the results are also listed. When you click on a specific type of malware, you can get more details about it.

Monitoring malware details

If you go to the **Assets and Compliance** section, you can get more information about the malware. To get more details regarding the malware, do the following:

1. Go to the **Assets and Compliance** section.
2. Click on a device collection, select a computer, and click on the **Malware Details** tab.

This tab will give you information about the threat name, detection time, category, severity, default action, state name, detection mode, and so on. You can also customize the view by adding and removing columns.

Monitoring Endpoint Protection details

IT administrators need to be able to quickly find out whether a computer is managed by the SCEP and the Endpoint Protection's policy name. To get this information, do the following:

1. Go to the **Assets and Compliance** section.
2. Click on a device collection, select a computer, and click on the **Endpoint Protection** tab.

Here, you can get very important information such as:

- Deployment information
- Remediation information
- Policy application information

Performing on-demand actions for the malware

Another very important functionality of Endpoint Protection is the on-demand scanning, that is, full or quick scanning. This gives commands to the SCEP client to first update the malware definition files and then initiate actions. To perform on-demand actions, do the following:

1. Go to the **Assets and Compliance** section.
2. From the navigation tree, choose **Overview** and select **Device Collections**.
3. Select the device collection managed by Endpoint Protection, and then select the client that you want to scan.
4. Right click on the client, select **Endpoint Protection**, and then you can select the full, quick, or download definitions.

The actions will not start right away but instead, they will start when the client receives the next policy. The default interval is defined in the client settings policy and is 60 minutes.

Reporting in Endpoint Protection

Endpoint Protection has six built-in reports. The reports allow IT administrators to go deep and gain more information regarding the malware. With the help of role-based authentication, you can assign reports to management personnel. These are the Endpoint Protection built-in reports:

- **Top users by threats**

  This is a list of users with the greatest number of detected threats. The report asks for a collection name and optionally asks for a start and end date. The report lists users by threat, incident count, number of computers, and when the threat was detected. You can go deep into the report by clicking on the username. This lists the computer name and the threat with the severity level of the malware, category, incident count, and detection date. If you want to get more information about the malware, click on the threat's name. This will display a report describing that particular theat.

- **User threat list**

  This is a list of the threats found under a particular user account. It is important and also useful to find the user who put a risk on the organization through their activities. You can also print the report that displays their account name and show it to the involved users and their managers.

- **Antimalware activity report**

  To view this report, you need to enter a device collection name for which you want to view information and also choose a start and end date. This report is an overview of the antimalware that is either removed from the computers in the collection or is quarantined.

- **Infected computers**

  This is a list of the computers that have had malware on them in a specific time frame. You can also enter the threat's name, the default action taken, and the infection status. Infection status is one of the three remediation states. The possible selections are:

    - Remediation fail
    - Remediation with pending actions
    - Remediated
    - Null

- **Infected computers report**

  For this report, you need to select a collection name and also choose the start and end dates. Moreover, you can select which cleaning action took place—whether it is cleaned, quarantined, removed, allowed, user specified, no action, blocked, or null. You can also select the previously mentioned remediation status. To go further into the report, you can enter the malware's name.

- **Dashboard report**

  For this report, you need to enter a device collection name first and the start and end dates. This report shows different pieces of Endpoint Protection information about the computers in the selected device collection. It also gives you a graphical overview of the state of Endpoint Protection for the collection.

The Endpoint Protection client

The Endpoint Protection client is the application found in the system tray, which is used by users to view the malware that is detected on their computer. When the client and the computer is in a healthy state, the icon is green. When malware is detected, the client changes color; it becomes red and it also flashes in the system tray to alert the user. Depending on the malware and its severity, a user can be asked to take action by clicking on **Clean Computer**. If the user doesn't take an action, the client itself determines what action is appropriate and applies it based on the antimalware policy.

Installing the Endpoint Protection client

You must distinguish the Configuration Manager client from the Endpoint Protection client. When you deploy the Configuration Manager client, the Endpoint Protection client is prestaged. The files are locally cached and the SCEP is installed only when the client settings are configured to enable the System Center Endpoint Protection client.

Understanding Endpoint Protection client settings

When you install System Center Endpoint Protection, you can choose from six configurable options. Multiple custom client settings can be created, multiple collections can be targeted, and you can give them different priorities and functionalities. The custom client settings always take priority over the default client settings. If a computer is a member of multiple collections targeted by different custom client policies, the custom policy with the highest priority wins. Here are the settings that you can configure:

- **Manage Endpoint Protection client on client computers**:

  This allows Configuration Manager to manage the SCEP client that is found on the computer. If the machine has an Endpoint Protection client and you set this setting to **True**, it will allow Configuration Manager to manage this SCEP client.

- **Install Endpoint Protection client on client computers**:

  This is used to control the installation of the Endpoint Protection client on client machines. If you set this to **False** and the setting from the first bullet to **True**, it will allow you to uninstall third-party antimalware software. If you set this to **True**, it will force the installation of the Endpoint Protection client agent.

- **Automatically remove previously installed antimalware software before Endpoint Protection is installed**:

  If you set this to **True**, it will uninstall antimalware software, such as McAfee, Symantec, and TrendMicro.

- **Suppress any required computer restarts after the Endpoint Protection client is installed**:

  Sometimes, the installation of the SCEP client agent requires a restart. If this is the scenario, you can set this to **True** in order to suppress a restart. This can be very useful for servers.

- **Allowed period of time users can postpone a requires restart to complete the Endpoint Protection client installation**:

  This setting defines how long the client can postpone the restart needed after the client installation.

- **Disable alternate sources for the initial definition update**:

  When this is set to **True**, it will force the first update of Endpoint Protection definitions to come from Configuration Manager rather than from other sources. When the Endpoint Protection client is installed before receiving its first policy, it doesn't know where to get its definition updates from; so, setting this option ensures that it polls only Configuration Manager for the definition updates.

Automatic removal of antimalware software

When you install the SCEP client, you can uninstall third-party antivirus software. It will allow the following antivirus software to be uninstalled:

- All Microsoft antimalware products, except Windows Intune and Security Essentials
- Symantec Antivirus Corporate Edition 10
- Symantec Endpoint Protection 11
- Symantec Endpoint Protection Small Business Edition 12
- MacAfee Virus Scan Enterprise Version 8
- Trend Micro OfficeScan

The antivirus software that is not listed must be uninstalled with a custom uninstaller. If you do not uninstall it first, it will leave your computer with two antivirus solutions, which can cause instability and performance loss.

Removing the Endpoint Protection client

If you need to remove the Endpoint Protection client, you have to apply a script to the machines where it is installed. The removal of SCEP is not automatic and if you disable the Endpoint Protection client agent settings, it will not remove the client. Even if you remove the Configuration Manager client, it will not remove the SCEP client. To remove the SCEP client, you must uninstall it manually from **Programs and Features** or execute this script:

```
scepinstall.exe /u /s
```

Delivering definition updates

When you configure a custom antimalware policy for Endpoint Protection, you must specify the definition update's source. There are five sources that you can choose from:

- Updates distributed from WSUS
- Updates distributed from Microsoft Update
- Updates distributed from Microsoft's malware protection center
- Updates distributed from Configuration Manager
- Updates from UNC file shares

Summary

In this chapter, we learned more about compliance settings and Endpoint Protection. With knowledge and creativity, compliance settings can give you feedback on the configuration and compliance of your Windows-based systems and mobile devices. Together with the remediation features, compliance settings can enforce compliance standards through the hierarchy. Compliance settings have a big impact on the companies in the area of configuration and compliance verification and enforcement from one single tool. Integrating System Center Endpoint Protection into Configuration Manager is a great feature that it offers. It consolidates security tasks together with client management and reduces cost. You can now simply enable the Endpoint Protection role within Configuration Manager and configure client and antimalware settings. In the next chapter, we will take a look at the **Software Library** section of the Configuration Manager console and see how to create packages and applications and how to distribute them to clients.

3

The Software Library

The biggest challenge in client and server administration is the management of the software components that are installed on them. This includes:

- Deploying software on servers and clients
- Updating the existing software
- Making an inventory of the installed software
- Uninstalling the software

In this chapter, we will take a look at how System Center Configuration Manager deals with software packages, and we will also see an example on how to deploy software on workstations.

Introducing packages

A package in Configuration Manager contains information about the software that will be installed. The information included in the software package is: name, version, manufacturer, language, and source files. Software packages can be created from a package definition file such as MSI, SMS, or a PDF file, or they can be created manually. Configuration Manager uses the MSI installation file to extract information from it to automatically input the information included in the package. Configuration Manager can create a package if the software doesn't have a package file. It can deploy executables, batch files, VBScript, JavaScript, and command files. Anything that can be executed can be put in a package. Programs on the other hand show the specifics of how the software is executed, and this is an optional part of the package. The package also consists of information about the security permissions and who has access to the software package and where it can be distributed. Packages are used when you want to deploy software to client machines.

Programs in Configuration Manager

Every package in Configuration Manager can contain one or more programs.
Programs specify what should be done on the client machine when the package
is deployed. When a package is deployed, programs in System Center Configuration
Manager will do one of the following:

- Do nothing
- Install software
- Distribute data
- Execute antivirus software
- Update the configuration

At least one program has to be contained in the package if the package has to
perform some actions. Otherwise, it will just point to the source file. The MSI files
provide six default programs when used for distribution:

- **Per-system attended**: This causes the installation of a program. It expects
  user interaction, and it is executed once for the system.

- **Per-system unattended**: This causes installation of a program, and it doesn't
  expect user interaction. It is also executed once for the system.

- **Per-system uninstall**: This uninstalls a program and is executed once for
  the system.

- **Per-user attended**: This causes installation of a program and also expects
  user interaction. It is executed once for the user that is targeted.

- **Per-user unattended**: This causes installation of a program, and it doesn't
  expect user interaction. It is also executed once for the targeted user.

- **Per-user uninstall**: This performs the uninstallation of the program and is
  executed once for the system.

Every program shows the command line used to execute the program in one of the
described methods.

Collections

A collection in Configuration Manager is a logical group of devices, users, or security
groups. In Configuration Manager, a collection can contain either users or machines
but it cannot contain both. A collection is a target for Configuration Manager's
functionalities. One of these functionalities is software distribution. Collections
can be static (defined by a specific resource) or dynamic (built by a query).

Distribution Points

A **Distribution Point** (**DP**) is a Configuration Manager server role and is used for storage of packages that are set for distribution. Clients connect to a distribution point and gather the source files of the installation.

Deployments

Deployments in Configuration Manager bring together all of the previously mentioned concepts. Deployment orders provide mechanisms that take a specific program from a package and provide it to a collection. It also specifies the distribution point when that package is deployed. Deployments can have three different states: available, required, or installed silently. In Configuration Manager 2012 R2, deployment is a general term and is used for different functionalities of Configuration Manager such as packages, applications, software updates, compliance settings, client agent settings.

Combining the use of packages, programs, collections, and deployments

A package can contain one or multiple programs. The package is later sent to the distribution point and deployed to a collection. This is a very powerful functionality, and this is demonstrated through an example: a specific application needs to be deployed on a collection. This is what you have to do:

- Create a package for the application and unattended installation
- Define a collection of the workstations that need to be targeted
- Create a deployment that brings all of these together

This deployment will bring together the package and the program to the collection and the distribution point that will deploy the package.

When combined, these concepts become important to deploy software to clients.

Creating a package

In this example, we will use 7-Zip, which can be downloaded from
`http://sourceforge.net/projects/sevenzip/`.

As an example of how to create a package with the packaging wizard, we will use the Windows installer distributable of 7-Zip to go through the process of creating a package from that definition file. Download the latest version of 7-Zip. To create the package in Configuration Manager, proceed with the following steps:

1. Download the 7-Zip installation file and put it at a location that can be accessed by the Configuration Manager server.

2. Open the Configuration Manager console and navigate to **Software Library | Overview | Application Management | Packages**. Then, navigate to **Create | Create package** from **Definition** from the ribbon bar. This will start the wizard:

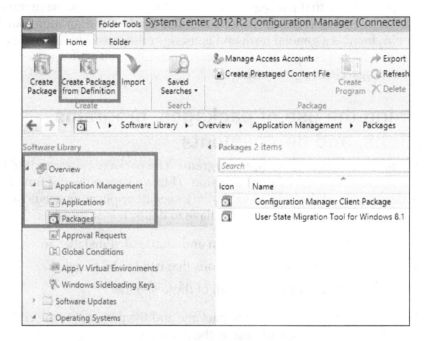

3. When you reach the **Create Package from Definition Wizard** page, click on **Browse...** and navigate to the MSI file. Click on **Next** to continue:

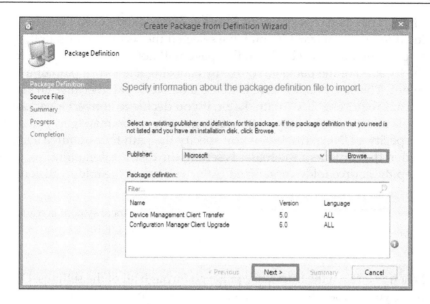

4. The next page in the wizard shows three ways to manage source files:

    ° **This package does not contain source files**

    ° **Always obtain source files from a source folder**

    ° **Create a compressed version of the source files**

In this example, we will use the second option, **Always obtain source files from a source folder**, and click on **Next** to continue:

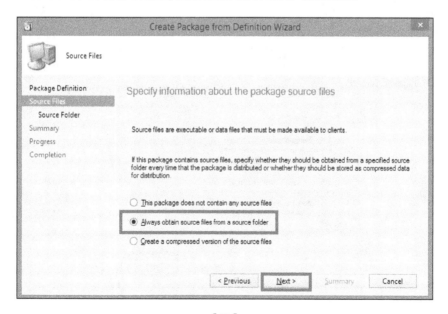

5. The wizard then checks for the location of the source files. This step is only included in the wizard if you have selected the second option in the previous step. If you haven't selected it, this page will not appear. You have to specify the location of the package source by choosing a network path or a local folder. The best practice here is to use a network path because an application always requires a UNC path. Later, if you decide to convert a package to an application with the help of the package conversion manager, you only need to specify a UNC path. When you specify the path to the source installation folder, the content of the folder is sent to the distribution point; so, try to keep the source folder organized. After you select the folder, click on **Next**.

 The Configuration Manager process runs as the local system account. You have to make sure that the computer account of the site server has read permissions of the source folder.

6. When you reach the **Summary** page, go through all of the settings. On this page, you can see the options you have chosen to create the package. The information that is displayed is the name of the package, how to handle source files, and the location of the source folder. Click on **Next** to create the package:

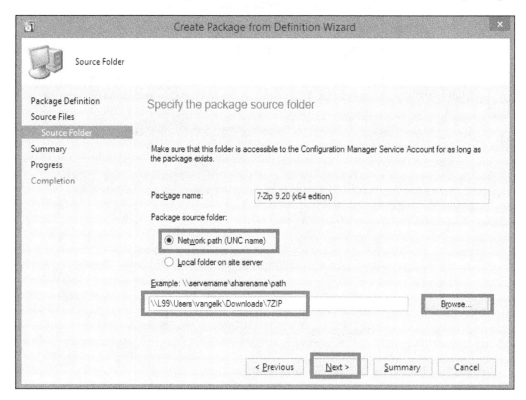

7. The wizard uses the information from the MSI file to create a set of installation options for the program.

Using MSI files for package definition greatly simplifies the creation process of the package because a lot of the information is extracted from the MSI file, which is otherwise provided manually. Whether you create the package manually or through a package-creating wizard, the files from the content source folder are taken and placed in the content store of the site that owns the package. You also need to send the content to all necessary distribution points to ensure that the content is available to target collections.

Package properties

After the package is created, you can view the properties of the package and program to check whether all settings are in order. Information from the **General** tab is helpful to anyone who has to choose a software installation from the application catalog or the software center. On the **Data Source** tab, you can see the package source location and the current source version. If the contents in the source folder are updated frequently, then make sure that the **update distribution points on a schedule** checkbox is enabled. When you schedule an update on the distribution point, Configuration Manager sends the contents from the source folder to the specified distribution points. If no changes were detected, nothing is re-sent. You can enable the following options in the data source tab as required:

- **Persist content in the client cache**: This option is used to ensure that the installation source remains in the local cache of the system. This option is great for software that might need to be executed again on a schedule.

- **Enable binary differential replication**: Use this replication for packages that contain large files.

- **Copy the content in this package to a package share on distribution point**: This feature enables System Center Configuration Manager 2012 R2 to have a single instance of the content. If you select this option to copy the content to a file share, Configuration Manager will copy all of the files and place them on a file share. If you want to deploy from a distribution point, you have to enable this option.

- **Disconnect users from distribution points**: When you make a deployment from a distribution point, the application might stop and hang in place, and this means that the target system has all of the files locked. You have to enable this checkbox and also configure the retry and notify options.

- **Distribution priority**: This option is used to control the order in which packages are sent to the distribution points.

- **Distribute the content for this package to preferred distribution points**: Every client has a preferred distribution point when it is in the boundary of a distribution point. In this case, when a client makes a request for a package that is not on the preferred distribution point, the content will first be pushed to the distribution point and then it will be sent to the client.

- **Prestaged distribution point settings**: This setting has the following options:

  ○ **Automatically download content when packages are assigned to distribution points**: This option causes the distribution point to not follow any prestaged content rules

  ○ **Download only content changes to distribution point**: This option makes you export the content and then extract the content manually on the distribution point for initial distribution. All future updates are only delta updates. A typical example of this is when you want to deploy, for example, Microsoft Office, because the installation is around 1GB. You can choose to transfer the installation manually. After the initial deployment, all other deployments function normally.

  ○ **Manually copy the content in this package to distribution point**: This setting blocks the copy process of the content to the distribution point and requires you to export the content and extract it to a different distribution point.

- **Operating system deployment settings**: This option allows you to enable multicast and encryption and allows only packages to be transferred via multicast.

The **Content Location** tab enables IT administrators to check the targeted distribution points and distribution point groups and also perform the following tasks:

- **Validate content**: This action makes Configuration Manager perform a hash check for the wanted package on a selected distribution point

- **Redistribute content**: This action confirms that all packages are on the targeted distribution point when needed

- **Remove content**: This action removes the content from a distribution point, and it can also be used to remove the content from all distribution points in a group

The security tab shows users and users' groups who have rights on the package.

Program properties

After you created the package, the next step will be to configure the program that the package will use. There are six programs for the package. All of the programs are automatically created if you use the create package from the definition wizard. For example, let's select a system-based unattended installation. This installation will deploy the 7-Zip installation on a per-system basis without any user interaction. Navigate to **Software** | **Library** | **Overview** | **Application Management** | **Packages**, right-click on the per-system unattended option and select the 7-Zip package. Then, open the **Properties** page. The properties for every program include the following tabs:

- **General**
- **Requirements**
- **Environment**
- **Advanced**
- **Windows installer**
- **Operations Manager Mode**

Every tab defines how the program will function. The **General** tab displays information gathered from the definition file. This information is as follows:

- **Name**: This field cannot be changed after populating it.
- **User description**: This field is a text field and is used to describe the program.
- **Command line**: This field gives the command line that will install the 7-Zip application. Here is an example:

```
msiexec.exe /q ALLUSERS="" /m MSIIMXSK /i "7z922.msi"
```

- **Start in**: This field shows either the absolute path to the program or the relative path to the distribution point you are installing from.
- **Run**: This drop-down option specifies whether the program will run:
    - **Normal**: This makes the program run on the system and program defaults.
    - **Minimized**: This makes the program run minimized only on the taskbar.
    - **Maximized**: This makes the program run maximized. This option is great when you want to catch the user's attention.
    - **Hidden**: This makes the program hide during installation, and you should use this for fully automated program deployment.

The installation process of 7-Zip with default values is as follows:

- **After installation**: This is a drop-down menu that shows what happens after the installation of the program finishes:
  - ° **No action required**
  - ° **Configuration manager restarts computer**
  - ° **Program controls restart**
  - ° **Configuration manager logs off user**

- **Category:** This is a drop-down selection used to organize programs in the application catalog

 When you enter a category, that category cannot be removed.

Creating a package with the new package wizard

Another application that is free is Microsoft Word Viewer, which is used to view or print Word documents. Follow these steps in order to create a package with the help of the create package and program wizard:

1. Navigate to **Software Library | Overview | Application Management | Packages**. Navigate to **Create | Create Package** from the ribbon bar:

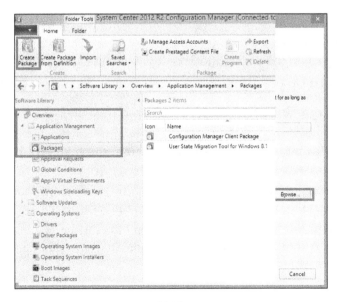

2. On the **Package** page, you have to specify several fields. These fields will be visible in the Configuration Manager console, software center, and application catalog. Check the checkbox named **Package Contains Source Files** and browse to the source file location. You can select a local path or a UNC path. If possible, always use UNC paths.

3. On the **Program Type** page, you have to choose between three options:

   ° **Standard program**: This setting is a standard program to deploy software.

   ° **Program for device**: This setting is used to create a package that is used for deployments on mobile clients.

   ° **Do not create a program**: This option is used to create packages in order to access the source files on a distribution point. This option can be used for OS deployment, running scripts, utilities, and so on.

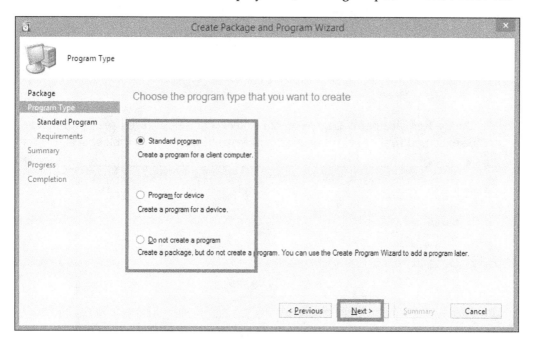

4. On the **Standard Program** page, you have to enter the required information, that is, the name and command line, or modify other required settings. Once you do this, click on **Next**:

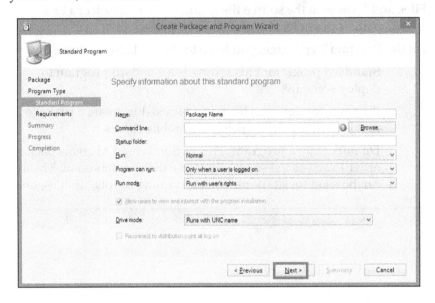

5. On the **Requirements** page, you can select whether another program must be executed first or set other platform restrictions such as disk space:

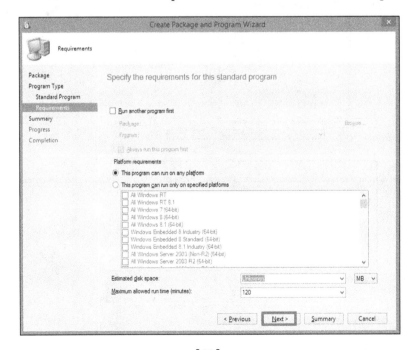

6. On the **Summary** page, check all of the settings and click on **Next**.

Custom packages

Most of the packages that many organizations need have package definition files because most of them have MSI files. You can manually create packages for those that do not have a package definition file but have setup files. You can also install an application with a batch file or a script. If you want to deploy more complex applications, use the unattended deployment of the application.

Repackaging software

There are packages that cannot be packaged using standard procedures. These packages are repackaged. Software repackaging converts the existing application installation to an MSI package. You can check out the following blogs for a list of packagers:

* http://itninja.com/software
* http://www.myitforum.com

One of the best known packagers can be found at the following link:

http://www.flexerasoftware.com/products/application-packaging/adminstudio-suite/

Avoiding common issues

When you create packages in Configuration Manager, you can always come against common issues. Most issues occur from low or no understanding of Configuration Manager options. A key point to always remember is that like any other software, Configuration Manager does what you configure it to do. If you deploy a package that is not configured the way it should be, you will not get the results you want. So, whatever you do, always test your configuration.

Testing packages

Every time you create a package, you must test it before deploying it. You can always expect undesired situations when deploying a package that wasn't tested to a collection that consists of hundreds of workstations. This is why the testing process can limit the risks that can occur from a misconfigured package.

To be able to test the packages, you will need a test environment. A test environment is a collection of laptops or desktops that represent systems from a production environment. If possible, you should separate your production environment from your test environment. If you are running a virtualized environment, you can always deploy several virtual machines and test the packages on them. Also, returning the virtual machine to a previous state is easier than on a physical machine. This is of great benefit when you want to test packages and go through several test iterations. One thing to consider is that in a virtual environment, you will not be able to test driver packages for physical machines. You will have to make a choice when to use a physical environment and when to use a virtual test environment. Always test on machines similar to the ones you have in production. The best practice is to use a mixture of virtual and physical machines. You should always consider what kind of tests you will run and make groups of tests with similar test conditions. The following are examples of groups of tests:

- What happens when you install a package when there is not enough space on the client?

- What happens when you deploy a package to a target system that is not supported?

- What happens when you deploy a program that has already been deployed on the target system?

- What happens when the packages have other requirements?

- What happens when the package is in conflict with other programs on the target system?

Identifying issues and potential failure proactively and testing them thoroughly will increase the chances of creating a great package.

Creating and managing applications

Applications and deployment types can help the administrators of Configuration Manager to easily manage and deploy different software types on the client machines. Configuration Manager 2012 R2 can deploy software to collections, both device and user collections.

Users can be associated with their devices. This is a user setting, and it is called a primary device. This setting allows you to deploy software specific to users' needs. This helps IT administrators control the applications that are installed on the user's primary device and on any other device that the user might work on in the future.

Application deployment is handled by deployment types. An application can have multiple deployment types.

About applications

Applications are containers that are used for software delivery. They contain information for applications. They also list the dependencies on other applications and check whether the specific application replaces an existing application. You can perform the following actions:

- Distribute application content to distribution points
- Deploy an application with the required or optional state to client devices or users
- Create a deployment type
- Simulate deployment
- Export an application
- Create a prestaged file and transport it to remote locations
- Set security scopes so that users have appropriate access to the application
- Monitor content distribution
- Monitor deployment status

About deployment types

Deployment types are a very important component of an application. A deployment type is a combination of a program and a package. The program contains the installation command line and requirements. The deployment type contains them all and more. This is a list of important information regarding deployment types:

- Content source location: The UNC path to the installation source
- Command lines for installation and uninstallation
- Detection methods: These are used to confirm whether an application is already installed, check for dependencies, and supersedence
- Configuration of user experience: This means to configure when to display user notifications
- Requirement rules: These are used to determine when to proceed with the installation
- Return code for success and failure
- Dependency information: This checks for applications that are dependent on other applications

You can create multiple deployment types for an application. If you have software that has both x86 and x64 installation files, the deployment type is created properly and the application is deployed. Then, the deployment types are checked to determine the best installation for the system.

The main user of a particular device is called a primary user. One device can have many primary users. You can define a primary user for a device during the deployment of an operating system from the configuration manager console, or it can be created automatically when someone logs on to the machine.

There are five deployment types available:

- **Microsoft application virtualization**: If you want to create virtual applications using the Microsoft App-V sequence, create an output file that contains the application information. You can use this deployment to import the manifest file to the configuration manager. The wizard to create the deployment type gives the result of the import, and the wizard information fields are populated from the file.

- **Windows installer**: This deployment is used for any Windows installer file that is the MSI file. Configuration Manager extracts information from the MSI file and then displays that information in the wizard.

- **Script installer**: This deployment type allows the IT administrator to specify a script that will be deployed on client machines, and it will execute the installation. This script can be a visual basic or a batch file.

- **Windows mobile cabinet**: Windows mobile cabinet or CAB files are files used mainly to deploy software to manage mobile devices. This deployment type is used to create deployment files for cabinet files. This deployment type gathers information from the CAB file and displays it in the wizard.

- **Nokia SIS file**: For this deployment type, you need the Nokia Symbian installation source file to populate fields in the wizard.

Requirements as a component of a deployment type

Requirements are a component of a deployment type. Requirements help decide whether a deployment type can be installed on a target system. If you don't have a requirement rule, this is fine as it is optional. In this case, the deployment type can be installed on any target system. Requirements are also used to determine which of the deployment types to install. For example, if you have an application with four different deployment types and the requirements for each, then all requirements are evaluated in the order of priority:

- OS: Windows 8, Architecture: x86, Primary User: true
- OS: Windows 8, Architecture: x64, Primary User: true
- OS: Windows 7, Architecture: x86, Primary User: true
- OS: Windows 8, Architecture: x86 or x64

So, let's say that the target operating system is Windows 8, it is x86, and the primary user is false. Then, the last condition will evaluate to true. Let's say that the operating system is Windows 7, it is x86, and the primary user is false. Then, none of the conditions will evaluate to true.

Global conditions

All requirements are defined with a global condition. A global condition is based on an operating system, memory, disk space, architecture, active directory site, and so on. You can use global conditions to create requirements for deployment types. Requirements are not a necessity for deployment types, such as:

- Operating system
- Memory
- Disk space
- Architecture
- Active directory site

Global conditions can be used to create requirements for deployment types. Needless to say, requirements are not mandatory for deployment types.

Detection methods

Detection methods help with the determination process if a deployment type is already installed on a device. They are mandatory and should be unique for the deployment type. If you want to use the deployment type properly, you have to define a detection method. When an application is subject to evaluation, the detection method checks to see whether the application is already installed on the target system. If the application is present on the target system and it is deployed as required, the Configuration Manager client will make an evaluation every week.

User Device Affinity

User Device Affinity is a new feature in System Center Configuration Manager 2012. It gives IT administrators the ability to associate users with a primary device. This is the device that the user uses on a daily basis. The relationship between users and devices is **N: M**, meaning a user can be associated with multiple devices and a device can be associated with multiple users. This means that Configuration Manager administrators can deploy an application to users without knowing on which device the specific user is working on. This gives Configuration Manager administrators more control in the deployment process of the application, because different rules can be created for User Device Affinity.

User Device Affinity is created in different ways:

- It can be created by importing a CSV file with columns for users and devices
- Users can specify their own device in the application catalog
- The Configuration Manager administrator can select it manually
- It can be set during operating system deployment
- It can be set during mobile device enrollment
- Configuration Manager might approve affinity between devices and users, and the site can determine affinities between users and devices according to the gathered information

An affinity can contain the following information:

- Single user to a single device
- Single user to many devices
- Many users to a single device

A deployment that consists of a package and a program is a preferred option than an application for the following scenarios:

- Scripts not used for software installation
- Scripts that do not require monitoring
- Software installations that are updated frequently
- Installed software with no detection method

Creating applications

This section will focus on the application creation process using the create application wizard. This wizard is a great approach to set up an application. However, keep in mind that several configuration options are only made available after you finish the wizard and create the application.

Creating a Windows Installer application

For the purpose of creating an application that uses Windows Installer, we will take the 7-Zip MSI file. Follow these steps to create a Windows Installer application:

1. Start the Configuration Manager console and go to **Software Library**.
2. Expand **Application Management** and right-click on the **Application** node.
3. Select **Create Application** from the menu.

The wizard starts with the **General** page that has two options:

- **Automatically detect the application information**
- **Manually define the information**

If you want to create an application for 7-Zip and use the existing Windows Installer content, then you have to perform the following:

1. Start the wizard and click on **Browse**. Go to the location of the MSI file. Remember that this path must be a UNC path. When the application is created, you also get a deployment type.
2. After selecting the file, click on **Next**. If you get a warning that the MSI file cannot be verified, ignore it. Click on **Yes** to import the file.
3. After this, the wizard gathers all the information from the MSI file.
4. Click on **Next** to see the results. The installation program is a default command line for an unattended Windows Installer installation. This information is used to create the deployment type.
5. The imported information from the MSI file can be minimal with only the name, program, and install behavior. If you want, you can edit this information. When you install 7-Zip, always use the **Install for system** option. IT administrators often make the deployment type **Install for system** if the resource is a device; otherwise, they use **Install for user**. This causes installations to fail if the user that is running the installation is not a member of the local administrators group.

6. The following screenshot gives you an example of the information you can add for 7-Zip. Click on **Next** to go the **Summary** page and review the information. Click on **Next** to create both the application and deployment types.

7. The last page from the wizard is the completion page, and it shows the successful completion of the application, or it can show errors with information about why the process terminated. Click on **Close** to finish the wizard.

You might have noticed that the wizard sets many options to their defaults. To view the details, select the application in the console and click on **Properties** from the ribbon bar.

Application properties

When you want to improve the functionality of a system, remember that it will bring complexity to the system. Applications in Configuration Manager are more complicated than packages and programs, but the benefit always outweighs the cost. Applications can be viewed as containers for the software deployment process. The information that is contained in an application provides user experience and application delivery.

Creating deployment types

Deployment types are an important part of an application. These next sections will focus on the creation process of a deployment type.

Creating a Windows Installer deployment type

To create a Windows Installer deployment type, perform the following:

1. Open the Configuration Manager console and go to **Software Library**.

2. Extend **Application Management**.

3. Right-click on the **Applications** node and select the 7-Zip application.

4. Right-click on the 7-Zip application and select **Create Deployment Type** from the menu:

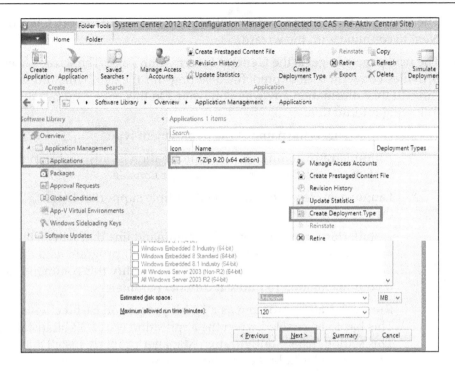

5. Click on the Add button.

6. When the **Create Deployment Type Wizard** page starts, choose Windows Installer as the type and browse to the MSI file and click on Next:

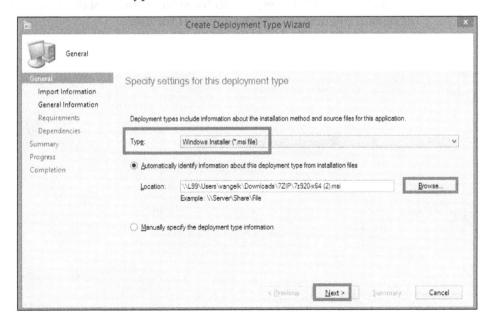

7. The **Import Information** window will show a successful import. Click on **Next** to continue with the wizard.

8. The next page you get is the **General Information** page. The wizard itself provides you with a set of predefined settings for the deployment type. You can edit this information any way you want. On this page, you can see the following information:

   ○ **Name**: This is the name of the deployment type.

   ○ **Administrator comments**: This information is only visible in the System Center Configuration Manager console.

   ○ **Languages**: Here, you can select multiple supported languages for the deployment type.

   ○ **Installation program**: This is the command line that will install the software. The default for a windows installer program uses the `/q` parameter for the silent install. You can modify this command line if your installation requires additional parameters.

   ○ **Run installation program as a 32-bit process on 64-bit clients**: This has to be enabled when the application uses a 32-bit installer. This setting helps Configuration Manager properly install and also uninstall a 32-bit application on a 64-bit system. By default, configuration manager doesn't use the `HKML\Software\WoW6432Node` registry path on a 64-bit system.

   ○ **Installation behavior**: This determines the rights used to install the software: **Install for user, Install for system,** and **Install for system if resource is device; otherwise install for user**:

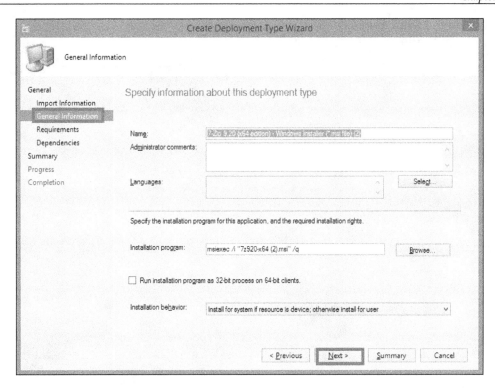

9. In the Requirements dialog, click on Add and choose the supported platforms:

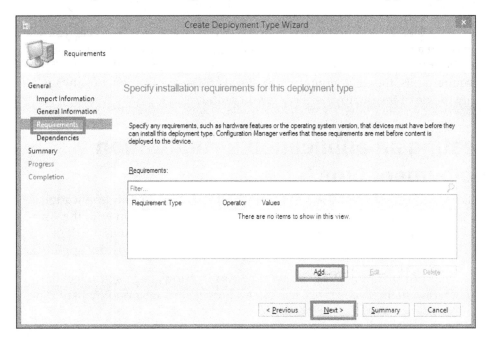

10. In the **Dependencies** dialog, you can view all of the software that this application is dependent on:

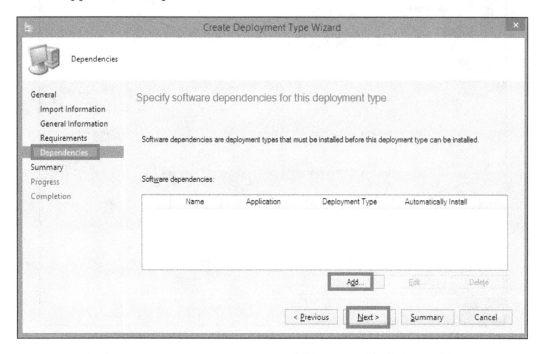

11. Click on **Next** to finish the wizard and create the deployment type.

The priority is an important feature of any deployment type. Whenever you want to deploy an application, the Configuration Manager client will evaluate the deployment types for that application in the order of priority. When a priority meets the requirements, the deployment type is used by the application. So, always set the priority to one of the deployment types you prefer.

Creating an application virtualization deployment type

This is the easiest way to create a deployment type. To create this application type, you can use the application wizard to create an application with the App-V deployment type, or you can choose an existing application and add a deployment type. Follow these steps to add a new deployment type to an existing application:

1. Go to **Application Properties** of the **Applications** page and select the **Deployment Types** tab. Click on **Add** to create a new deployment type.

2. For the deployment type, use **Microsoft Application Virtualization**. Browse to the location of the `.xml` file for App-V.

3. A message will be shown for a successful import. Click on **Next** to continue with the wizard.

4. The next page is a **General Information** page. An installation command is not required for the App-V application. Here, you can modify the information and click on **Next** to continue with the wizard.

5. In the **Requirements** page, you can see all of the requirements for this App-V application. This information is also included in the `.xml` file you previously imported. You can also click on **Add** to add additional requirements.

6. Click on **Next** on all pages that follow to complete the wizard.

Create an application that installs both the x86 and x64 versions of the App-V client. You have to create a dependency for the new App-V application. This will make sure that the client is installed prior to the application installation.

7. You can review the information in the content tab and check whether the application requirements were successfully imported from the manifest file. This tab displays the following information:

   ° **App-V manifest location**: This is the UNC path to the App-V application manifest file. This is a read-only location. In order to update the source location for this manifest file, click on **Update Content** from the deployment type properties.

   ° **Persistent content in the client cache**: If this setting is enabled when the application is deployed, all of the client machines will keep the installation source in the local configuration manager cache.

   ° **Enable peer-to-peer content distribution**: This enables peer-to-peer computing.

   ° **Load content in the App-V cache before launch**: If this setting is disabled and the download content option is enabled, the configuration manager client will get the content and store it in the local cache. If this setting is enabled and when content is downloaded, the configuration manager client will call the App-V command and preload the content to the App-V cache. This procedure has a problem: when this option is disabled and software is downloaded to configuration manager cache, the client doesn't execute the software until the cache is cleared. If this happens, the launch will fail. Best practice is to enable this option to always precache the application to the App-V cache.

- ○ **Deployment options**: If the client is on a gigabit network or any fast network, you can configure the application to always be streamed from the distribution point.

- ○ **Allow clients to use a fall back source location for content**: If the client cannot locate the content for the deployment, this checkbox allows the client to search for other locations. In order to allow clients to access the source from a different boundary group, the boundary group properties tab from the distribution point must be configured to allow fallback source location for the content.

8. Another specific tab for the App-V deployment type is the **Publishing** tab. You can use this tab to select which icons to publish to the end user.

9. In the **Requirements** tab, you can use the **Add** button to add a new requirement. In the **Create Requirements** dialog, you can select a category of users and verify that the condition for the primary device is true.

Creating a script-based deployment type

The term "script" is always associated with something that is written in PowerShell, VBScript, or any scripting language. There is also something called script-based installer. It can be `.exe`, `.bat`, `.com`, `.vbs`, or any other command type that can be run from a command line. This section discusses the process of creating another deployment type to an existing application. The creation process is very similar to the creation process of a Windows installer-based deployment type. To create a script-based deployment type, follow these steps:

1. Go to **Application Properties** and select **Deployment Types**. Click on **Add** to create a new deployment type.

2. For the type of deployment, select **Script Installer (native)**.

3. When you choose this, the source location is disabled. Click on **Next** to go to the **General Information** page.

4. Click on **Next** to go to the **Content** page. When using a script to install software, there are no universal install arguments for all executable files. So, the best practice is to work with the application vendor and request a MSI file or documentation on the right install/uninstall arguments. If you don't know the install arguments, you can leave them empty.

5. The **Detection Method** page will prompt for the creation of a valid detection method. If you use a MSI file, you get the detection method for free based on the Windows installer product type code. Click on the **Add Clause** button and select **File System** as the setting type. Click on **Browse** and go to the executable file.

It is often helpful to combine several applications in a single installer. This is called a wrapper. Wrappers must be created with caution, especially in the area of detection methods.

Checking whether a file exists on a specified path is a very simple task. This option only checks whether the file exists. You can also enable it to look for a specific date or version.

6. The **Requirements** page is the same as the one in the previous screenshot. Here, you can also configure global conditions. If you leave this option blank, it means that the installation will install on all client operating systems.

7. The dependency, summary, and progress pages from the wizard are the same as the ones in the wizard for a Windows installer-based application.

The process for creating a deployment type for a script-based installer is similar to the process of creating a deployment type for a Windows installer. You need to create detection methods and command-line arguments for installation and uninstallation of the application.

Creating detection methods

This section will focus on more detailed configuration of detection methods. It will help IT administrators understand the importance of a properly configured detection method. The goal of a detection method is to check whether specific software is installed on a target system. When an application is deployed on a target collection, every member of the target collection is evaluated on a regular interval.

This evaluation is called application deployment evaluation cycle and can be triggered from the client machine or configured in the client settings. If an application is not installed on the target device and the application deployment evaluation checks this state, it will launch a reinstallation process of the application.

Detection methods are very important because they can provide reports of the current state of the application on target systems. Detection methods have to be configured properly; otherwise, it might initiate a reinstallation of applications. Incorrect detection methods lead to an incorrect application state, and this leads to repeated attempts of application reinstallation.

Detection methods for a Windows Installer application

Applications that use the Windows installer have a very simple detection method. It uses the Windows installer application product code. If you choose the create application wizard or create deployment type wizard with the Windows installer application option, this detection method is automatically created and configured to use the Windows installer product code.

When you launch a wizard to create a Windows installer deployment type, it saves you some steps, but it can also cause problems in the future. If you work with special case installers, you might consider adding additional detection clauses in the detection method. These are the basic steps to create a Windows installer detection method:

1. From the Deployment Type properties, select the Detection Method tab and click on Add Clause.

2. Choose the Setting type; in this case, it is **Windows Installer**, and click on Browse.

3. Go to the location of the MSI file and click on **Open**. You can see the product code.

4. Click OK to save the detection code.

Other detection methods

There are built-in methods based on filesystem and registry properties besides the Windows installer detection method. These are the steps to create a filesystem-based detection method:

1. From the **Deployment Type** dialog, select **Detection Method** and click on **Add Clause**.

2. Choose the setting you want; in this case, it is **File System** and click on **Browse**.

3. On the **Browse File System** page, browse the computer that you have administrative rights to and click on **Connect**. Expand the computer information and find the desired file.

4. The **Detection Rule** dialog will show the file and folder information populated.

5. Information is automatically populated based on the file selected. It shows that the application will be looked for at the program files' 7-Zip folder. You can see the option, this file or folder is associated with a 32-bit application on 64-bit system. This means that the detection method will look in the 32-bit file location, and if it can not be found, it will look at the 64-bit location on a 64-bit system.

To create a registry-based detection method, perform the following:

1. From the **Deployment Type** properties, select the **Detection Method** tab and click on **Add Clause**.

2. Choose the setting you want; in this case, it is **Registry** and click on **Browse**.

3. Select the appropriate registry key or value and click on **OK**.

The process of detection method creation is straightforward. The only challenge is to determine which detection rules to create for the deployment type. You can group different clauses and also use the AND and OR connectors.

Custom script detection methods

This is the final detection method we will cover in this section. When using custom scripts, you can have endless possibilities. For most of the applications, you can use some of the standard detection methods: Windows installer, file, or registry. Sometimes, you will encounter applications that will require a different detection method.

If this is the case, then you need to configure a custom script that Configuration Manager will use to detect if that software is installed. When you configure custom script, always configure a return code. If you do not, Configuration Manager will configure a return code and then will treat it as not installed.

Custom detection methods with PowerShell

From the deployment type dialog, enable the detection method option to create a custom script and click on **Edit**. Select PowerShell as the script type. In this case, you might have to use client settings to adjust the PowerShell execution policy. The following PowerShell script is a simple script that checks for the existence of a file and verifies its version. If all tests pass, a simple text is written as an output. This text means that the file was found:

```
$strFilePath = "c:\Program Files\7-Zip\7zG.exe"
if (test-path) ($strFilePath))
{
$file = get-childitem $strFilePath | select *
if ($file.VersionInfo.ProductVersion -eq "9.22 beta")
{
write-host "Version Exists"
}
else
{
#version does not exist
}
}
else
{
#file doesn't exist
```

Managing applications

Applications are a very important part in System Center Configuration Manager 2012 and 2012 R2. This is why we went deep into the process of application creation and application properties. The next sections will describe additional properties and some features in order to use the maximum potential of applications.

Dependencies

Many applications require some prerequisites to be met before their installation. For example, many Microsoft products require the .NET framework to be present on the system.

In some applications, there is a mechanism to install all prerequisites with a single click. However, this mechanism is not smart because it will reinstall that prerequisite even if it is present on the system.

Dependencies in System Center Configuration Manager 2012 R2 are smart. When an application has a dependency, both the detection and requirement rules are executed in order to determine which deployment type to use. If the application has a prerequisite and the prerequisite is present on the target system, Configuration Manager will skip the installation to check all additional prerequisites. After it finishes with the prerequisites check, it will initiate the application. Here are some things regarding dependencies to keep in mind:

- An application can be dependent only on an application; it cannot be dependent on a package or a program.
- A package or a program cannot be dependent on an application.
- When you deploy an operating system, only application dependencies are checked. If you have program and package dependencies, you have to execute them separately.
- There is no specific order in which dependencies are checked.
- Dependency groups can be created for application requirements. When an application from the dependency group is installed on the target system, the requirement is satisfied.

If you have problems implementing the previously mentioned constraints, you can create a task sequence. A task sequence is mainly used for operating system deployment, but you can use it to create a generic task sequence to install software in a defined order.

 Task sequences can only be deployed on devices.

As an example of dependencies, we will take the installation of the Configuration Manager console. A prerequisite for the Configuration Manager console is the .NET framework 4.0. You can proceed with the following steps to create the dependency:

1. Go to the **Deployment** tab in the Configuration Manager console and select the **Dependencies** tab.
2. Click on **Add** to display the **Add Dependency** page.
3. Enter a group name for the installation and click on **Add** to display the **Specify Required Application** page.
4. Select the application and click on **OK**.

5. This shows the dependency information.

6. Auto-install is checked by default. This allows you to deploy software automatically on the target system.

7. Click on **OK** on the **Add Dependency Wizard** page and then again click on **OK** to save the deployment and the application.

Now, whenever you deploy the Configuration Manager console, Configuration Manager will install .NET Framework 4.0 automatically if it is not previously installed on the target device.

With this version of Configuration Manager, simply create a dependency from the App-V application to the App-V client installation application so that if the client does not already exist, it will be installed just in time for the App-V application.

Revision history

Revision history is a new feature in Configuration Manager 2012 and 2012 R2. Every time you modify an application, Configuration Manager creates a revision of that application. You can easily go back to a previous application configuration. What really happens in this process is that Configuration Manager makes a copy of the state and assigns it the latest number.

Only the last revision is currently referenced. You can select and also delete any revision that doesn't have a reference. Every primary site has a maintenance task that removes any revision not referenced and at least 60 days old.

To go back to a previous version, select the desired version in the console and click on **Restore**. Older versions have references too. You can see the revision to identify the reference and then go to the reference and reconfigure it to a newer version if you like. Note that you cannot remove a revision if it is referenced at the moment. Revision history is a distribution point content.

 Every time you change the source path of the application, the revision history will grow. As long as the state is present in the revision history, this space will remain in the distribution point too.

When you have completed the testing process and you are ready to deploy the application in production, consider implementing a process to clean up old revision history states.

Exporting and importing applications

System Center Configuration Manager 2012 R2 has a mechanism that allows you to export different objects from the administration console and import them in different infrastructures. This is a great way to migrate objects between two different infrastructures. In order to export an object, perform the following steps:

1. Open the **Configuration Manager** console and go to **Software Library** and select the **Applications** node.

2. Select any number of applications, right-click on them, and select **Export**.

3. Enter the path to store the export and be sure to include the `.zip` file extension. With this option, you can export dependencies, supersedence relationships, and global conditions. Also, you can export content for all of the selected applications and dependencies.

4. Go through the rest of the process.

5. With the application exported, you can transfer it to another infrastructure and import it there.

Superseding applications

Supersedence is instrumental when you want to upgrade to a new version of an application. For example, you have an application that you have previously deployed to multiple collections. There is a new version released of this application and you create a new application in Configuration Manager with the new version. After this, you can supersede the first application with the second. What you have to do next is deploy the new application on the targeted collections.

If you superseded an application that was deployed as a required application, then the redeployment will cause this application to re-install. If you have checked the **Uninstall** checkbox, Configuration Manager will uninstall the previous version on the target device first and then install the new version. If this checkbox is not checked, Configuration Manager will execute the new deployment type without uninstalling the previous application. This process will upgrade the previous installation.

If you have multiple deployment types in either the previous or the new application version, you can choose one of the old deployment types and the new deployment type to join them together and then determine which of the deployment types should run together.

You do not have to redeploy old versions of software just to take advantage of supersedence. If you have a version of an application and this application is in production, but you have just installed Configuration Manager in your infrastructure, you can create two applications. The first one will be the old one and the second one will be the new one. The second one supersedes the first one. This way, when you deploy the new application, it will detect that the first is installed on the target collection and will act according to the supersedence rules.

Application retirement and deletion

When you no longer have to create new deployments for an application, you can right-click on that application and select **Retire**. When an application is retired, you cannot create deployments for that application unless you reinstate it. When you retire an application, the targeted collections are not affected.

You can also delete an application. To do this, first you have to remove all references to it. Remember that you can export an application and store it for later use.

Package conversion

Package Conversion Manager (**PCM**) is a Microsoft feature for System Center Configuration Manager that you can download from the official site. This feature can help you with the migration process of Configuration Manager 2007 packages and programs the new application model. You can read more about this feature at the following link:

```
http://technet.microsoft.com/en-us/library/hh531583.aspx
```

Operating System Deployment

Whenever you want to deploy a new operating system into your organization, whether it is small or large, it is a large process that can cause implications. You have to properly plan and execute the move to your new operating system so that it minimizes the extra work, business continuity, upset users, and data loss. Beginning with Configuration Manager 2007, a new feature was introduced called **Operating System Deployment (OSD)**. In the newest edition of Configuration Manager, the 2012 R2 version, this functionality has improved greatly.

OSD is a whole process to deploy operating systems to new or existing machines. As there is an example of a Windows 8.1 deployment at the end of the section, from now on, I will use Windows 8.1 as a term when referring to an operating system. At the very core, OSD delivers a new instance of Windows to a Windows-compatible machine. It might sound simple but it is not. Mass delivery of a Windows operating system is nothing new, because there have been third-party tools on the market that organizations have been using to create an image of a system and copy it to other systems. The following features of OSD make it different from these tools:

- OSD automates the entire process, beginning from image creation and maintenance to the actual deployment to a machine

- OSD is an entire process that allows you to define custom actions before the image is applied to the system such as partitioning and BIOS updates and custom actions after the image is deployed such as software updates and application deployment

- OSD is integrated in System Center Configuration Manager 2012 R2, and it can take advantage of other features of the product such as software distribution, software updates, and reporting, all from a single integrated management console

In the next example, we will see how to use System Center Configuration Manager 2012 R2:

1. Go to the **Software Library** section of the console and expand **Operating Systems**. Right-click on **Operating System Images** and click on **Add Operating System Image**:

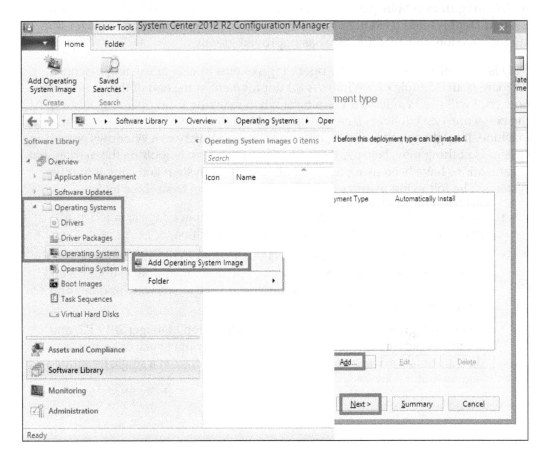

2. On the first page of the **Add Operating System Image Wizard** page, you have to point to the **Install.WIM** file located in the sources folder of the extracted Windows 8.1 ISO:

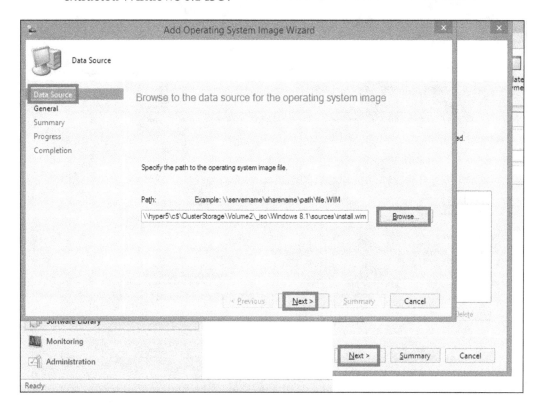

3. On the **General** page of the wizard, enter the name, version, and comments. This information is only descriptive. Click on **Next**.

4. Review the settings on the **Summary** page and finish the import.

5. After the import is finished, right-click on the image in the Configuration Manager console and click on **Distribute Content**, or the same from the ribbon bar, to distribute it to the distribution points:

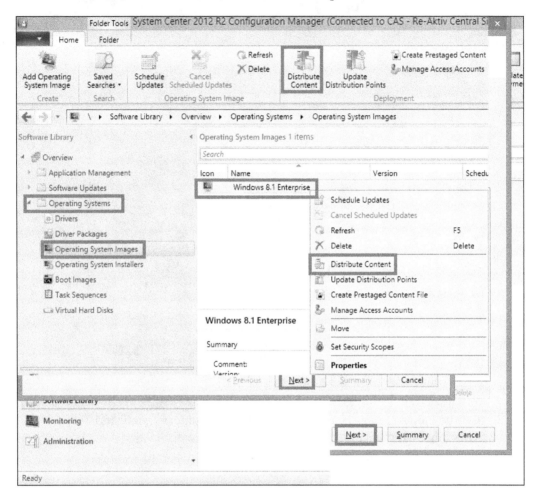

6. On the **Content Destination** page of **Distribute Content Wizard**, click on **Add** to add the distribution point servers:

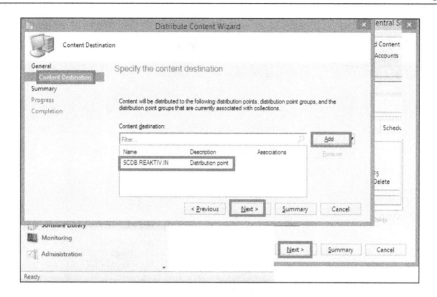

7. Go to the **Software Library** section of the Configuration Manager console, expand **Operating Systems**, and right-click on **Task Sequence** to create a new task sequence:

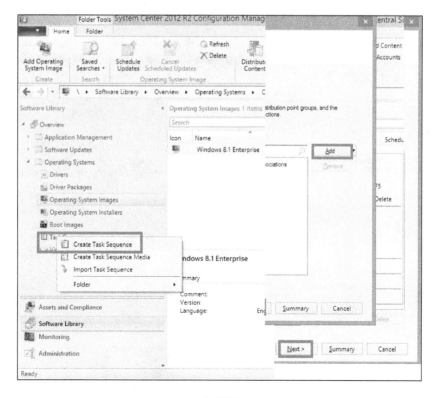

8. This will launch **Create Task Sequence Wizard**. On the first page of the wizard, choose **Install an existing image package**:

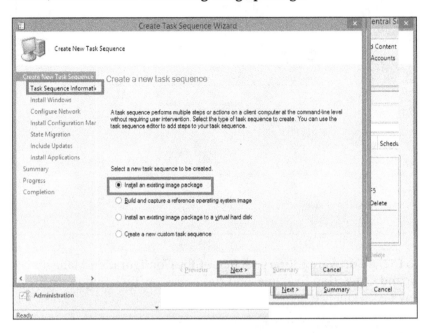

9. On the next page of the wizard, enter the name of the task sequence and select the boot image by clicking on the **Browse...** button to select the boot image from the list:

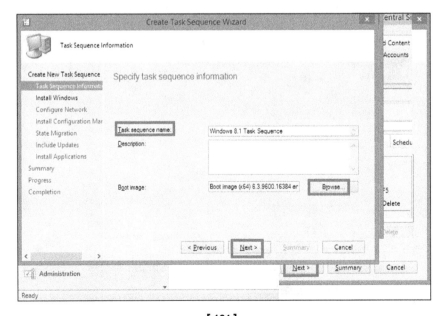

10. On the next page of the wizard, you have to select the image that was imported earlier. Click on **Browse...** and select it from the list. At the bottom of the page, select **Enable the account and specify the local administrator password**:

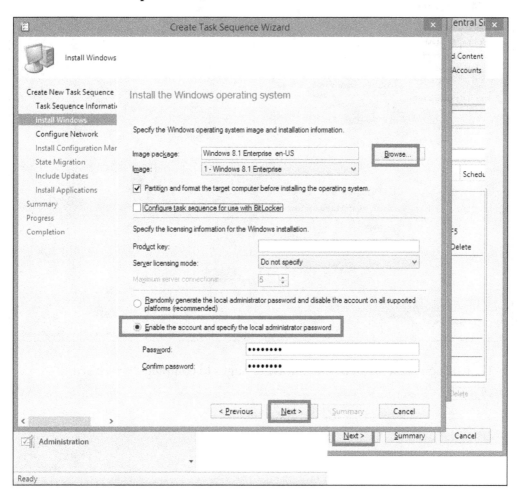

11. On the networking page, you can select a domain or workgroup to join:

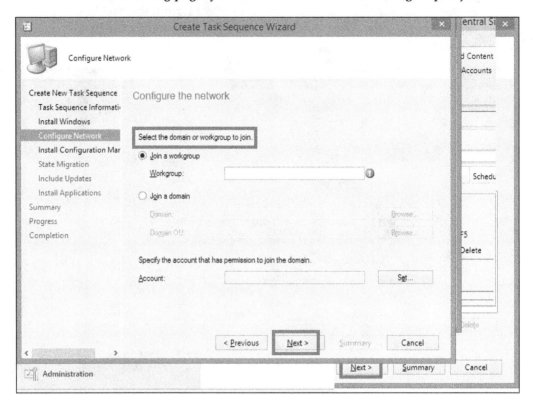

12. Click on **Next** on all of the following pages to complete the wizard.

13. What you have to do next is deploy the task sequence to a collection of devices. To do this, right-click on the **Task Sequence** option and click on **Deploy**:

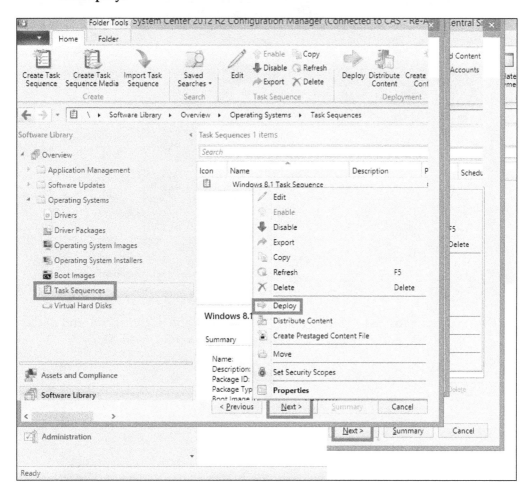

14. In the first step, you have to select the collection to which the sequence will be deployed:

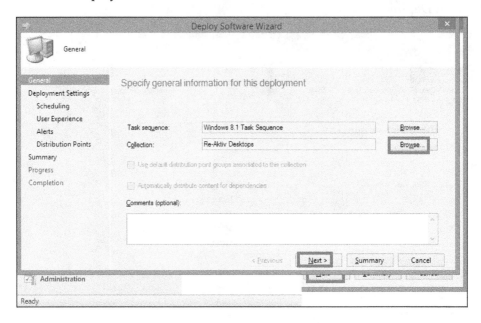

15. On the **Deployment Settings** page, select **Available** for **Purpose**, and at the bottom, select **Configuration Manager clients, media and PXE**:

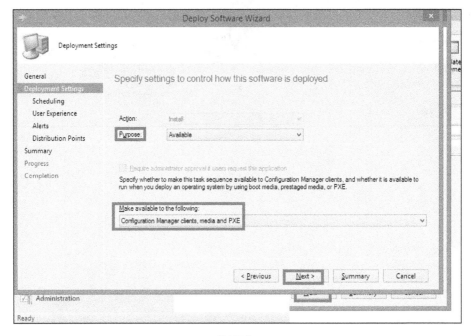

16. Click on **Next** on the following pages to complete the wizard.

This completes the creation of a task sequence. The next thing you have to do is boot a machine and choose the PXE boot as the boot device to start downloading the `boot.wim` file from Configuration Manager.

Summary

This chapter explained the different ways that you can deploy software and how to use System Center Configuration Manager to do this. It explained how different Configuration Manager components are combined and how they provide a software deployment solution. It also gives examples on how to create packages with and without definition files. It also explained what programs and packages are and how to configure them and avoid making errors while configuring them. Furthermore, the chapter gave an overview on what applications are and how to create them in Configuration Manager, make deployment types, and create different detection rules.

4
Reporting in Configuration Manager

Reporting is used when you want to analyze the data that is collected by System Center Configuration Manager 2012 R2. The product itself gives a wide range of predefined reports out of the box, which are more than enough to meet your demands. The product also allows you to create custom reports. In order to create a custom report, you need to know what data you want to show in your report and where to find the data in the Configuration Manager database. You access this data by constructing a SQL query, which you then use to create your report. In this chapter, we will see how to use the reporting section of System Center Configuration Manager. The chapter also concentrates on how to create a report in a secure manner and custom reports on demand.

SQL Server Reporting Services

SQL Server Reporting Services (**SSRS**) is a SQL Server functionality that was introduced way back with the 2000 edition of SQL Server. SSRS provides a full range of ready-to-use tools and services to help you create, deploy, and manage reports for your organization. Reporting Services includes programming features that enable you to extend and customize your reporting functionality. The integration between Configuration Manager and SSRS was first introduced in the 2007 version of Configuration Manager. For Configuration Manager 2012 and 2012 R2, SSRS is the only reporting option. SSRS has many features that give it advantages over other reporting tools. Here are the advantages of SSRS:

- It uses a standardized report system.

- SSRS **report definition language** (**RDL**) is stored in the XML format. This allows easy backup of the RDL files and easy migration between reporting servers.

- It has high performance, availability, and scalability.

- It allows you to build ad hoc reports.

- It has a lot of enhancements such as report subscription and report caching.

- It provides interactive features in the report template. For example, users can influence the appearance of a report and the data it contains by typing or selecting a value for a parameter before running the report; a user can also show or hide items in a report and click on links that go to other reports or web pages. Reporting Services also provides a document map that acts like a table of contents; a user can click on items in the document map to jump to areas within a report.

- It allows you to export reports to many different formats.

- It has interactive sorting capabilities.

Implementing SQL Server Reporting Services

This section will explain how to implement SSRS properly. To use the reporting section in Configuration Manager 2012 R2, you must first install SSRS.

SSRS requirements

In order to implement SSRS for System Center Configuration Manager, you need to have SQL Server 2008 SP1 or higher running on a Windows Server x64-based operating system. Additional information about supported SQL Server versions for Reporting Services Point can be found at the following link:

```
http://technet.microsoft.com/en-us/library/hh338695
```

You need to have a supported version of SSRS. All the supported versions can be found at the following link:

```
http://technet.microsoft.com/en-us/library/gg682077.aspx#BKMK_
SupConfigSQLDBconfig
```

SQL Server Reporting Services can be installed on the central administration site or any primary site in the hierarchy. If you install SSRS on the central administration site, it will enable reporting on all data and activities initiated from the central administration site. If you install SSRS on a primary site, it will allow you to report on data and activities initiated from that site. A best practice is to install Reporting Services Point on the top of your hierarchy. Next, you have to determine whether to install SSRS on the Configuration Manager database server or on a separate server.

There are advantages and disadvantages for both options:

- **SSRS on a Configuration Manager database server**: This is a fairly simple approach and requires no additional licensing. If you are running a virtual environment, you can increase the performance of the server by increasing the CPU and memory parameters on the virtual server if there are enough resources left on the physical machine. If you are installing SSRS on the database server, you should install it as a separate named instance. SSRS can also be installed on a default instance as the Configuration Manager database. Moving the databases to another server is very easy. To do this, you can use the guide at the following link:

  http://technet.microsoft.com/en-us/library/ms156421.aspx

- **SSRS on a dedicated server**: If you have large Configuration Manager sites that need higher performance, and if they can impact the Configuration Manager database server, you might choose a dedicated server for SSRS. To limit wide-area network traffic, the best practice is to deploy the SSRS server close to the Configuration Management database server. This way, you can fine tune the SSRS server without impacting the database server. The disadvantage is that you need additional servers and licenses. For more information on SSRS and reporting, you can visit the following link:

  http://technet.microsoft.com/en-us/library/hh394138.aspx

SQL Server Reporting Services installation

After you decide which deployment option you will choose, the next step is to install SSRS itself. In order to use SSRS in Configuration Manager, you must install it in the native mode. To do this, follow the guide at:

http://msdn.microsoft.com/en-us/library/ms143711.aspx

After the installation, you have to determine whether SSRS functions normally. To do this, follow the guide at:

http://msdn.microsoft.com/en-us/library/ms143773.aspx

After installing SSRS and confirming that it functions correctly, you can install and configure System Center Configuration Manager's Reporting Services Point role. To check whether SSRS is working properly, perform the following:

- Open a browser and enter http://reportserver/reports
- Open a browser and enter http://reportserver/

In order to do this, you have to follow these steps:

1. Open the Configuration Manager console and go to the **Administration** section.

2. Select the available server to use as a site system and choose the **Create Roles Wizard** option and select **Specify a FQDN** for this site system for use on the Internet.

3. Click on **Next** and then select **Reporting Services Point** as a system role.

4. On the **Specify Reporting Services Settings** page, verify that the site server and database names are correct. In the folder settings, the folder name corresponds to `ConfigMgr_<site code>.>`. You have to use an account that has administrative rights to the SSRS instance and choose **Use Windows Credentials** to connect to the data source.

5. On the **Summary** page, verify that the settings are correct and click on **Next**.

SSRS configuration

With SSRS installed and the Reporting Services Point role configured, it's time to implement access rights. There are several steps that you need to perform so that users can access Reporting Services for Configuration Manager. They will be discussed later. SSRS security can also be configured either from the Configuration Manager console or from SSRS Report Manager.

Role-based access control

Role assignments determine access to items that are stored on the report server. Configuration Manager SSRS security must be configured through the Configuration Manager console. System Center Configuration Manager will overwrite any SSRS permissions that have been granted outside of the Configuration Manager console. This is what you have to do to create a role assignment:

*   **A securable item**: This is an item that requires controlled access. It can either be a folder, a report, or some other resource.

*   **User or a group account**: This is an account that can be authenticated with either Windows security or any other authentication methods.

*   **Role definition**: This is a set of tasks.

The scope of a role can be either system- or item-specific. They are different in the following way:

- A system-scoped role is applied to the whole SSRS instance.
- An item-scoped role is applied to a specific folder or report. An item-specific role is dependent on the role assignment.

The following table provides the predefined roles in SSRS:

Predefined Role	Scope	Description
Content Manager	Item	This consists of all item-level tasks. Users assigned to this role have full permission to manage report server content, including the ability to grant permissions to other users and define the folder structure for storing reports and other items.
Publisher	Item	Users assigned to this role can add items to a report server; this includes creating and managing folders that contain these items.
Browser	Item	Users assigned to this role can run reports, subscribe to reports, and navigate through the folder structure.
Report Builder	Item	Users assigned to this role can create and edit reports in Report Builder.
My Reports	Item	Users assigned to this role can manage a personal workspace to store and use reports and other items.
System Administrator	System	Users assigned to this role can enable features and set defaults, set site-wide security, create role definitions in SQL Server Enterprise Management Studio, and manage jobs.
System User	System	Users assigned to this role can view basic information about the report server such as the schedule information in a shared schedule.

SSRS should not be configured outside Configuration Manager because Configuration Manager will sync role-based administration settings to SSRS.

Accessing SSRS Point

After Reporting Services Point is enabled, you need to determine whether the proper security groups can access the reports. To do this, follow these steps:

1. Open the report server in a browser. The URL to the report server is
   `http://<reportserver>/reports`.

2. A folder should exist beneath the home page with the name
   `ConfigMgr_<site code>`. This is the folder where the ConfigMgr site server reports are located.

3. Click on **ConfigMgr_<site code>** and select **Properties** and then **Security**.

4. To allow an Active Directory group, click on **New Role Assignment**.

Data sources

A data source is the connection between your report and the SQL Server database. The data source is important for the execution of the report and the return result set. Under Configuration Manager's site server report folder, there is a data source named **GUID**. If the **GUID** data source is renamed or deleted, Configuration Manager reporting will no longer function.

Backing up SSRS

Backing up SSRS is very important because the Configuration Manager backup task does not back up the SSRS database. If the SSRS database is not backed up and the SSRS server fails, you will have to reinstall the server and recreate all of the custom reports. This is what you have to do in order to back up the SSRS database configuration and reports:

- **Schedule a backup of the report server database**: The application data is stored in the `Reportserver` and `Reportservertempdb` databases, which are located on the SSRS reporting server instance. Use the SQL Server backup task to schedule a backup.

- **Back up SSRS encryption keys and archive the file in a safe location**: The encryption keys contain the secure credentials and connection information. They are essential when restoring reporting services or migrating them to a new server. There are two ways to back up the encryption keys:

- ° **Reporting services to the Configuration Manager**: Connect to the proper SSRS instance and select **Encryption Keys**. Click on **Backup** in the upper-right corner of the dialog window and select the **Backup Encryption Key** dialog box. Then, select the file location and password and click on **OK**.

- ° **RsKeyMgmt.exe**: This is a utility that runs as a command locally on the report server. The syntax is as follows:

  ```
  Rskeymgmt -e -f<filename> -p <password>
  ```

- **Backup any custom report data files and report models that you have created with Report Designer or Report Builder**: These files include report definition files, report model files, shared data source files, data view files, data source files, report server project files, and report solution files. Remember to back up any script files that you have created for administration or deployment tasks.

- **Backup the configuration files that SSRS uses to store application settings**: Back up these files when you first configure the server and again after deploying any custom extensions. The SSRS configuration files that have to be backed up are as follows:

  - ° `Rsreportserver.config`

  - ° `Rssvrpolicy.config`

  - ° `Rsmgrpolicy.config`

  - ° `Reportingserviceservice.exe.config`

  - ° `Web.config` for the report server and report manager `asp.net`

  - ° `Machine.config` for `asp.net`

- Back up any of your custom views and stored procedures that you have created for your custom reports.

 To avoid using disk space after you install SSRS and configure backups, change the database recovery mode from full to simple. This setting will save the disc space regarding the transaction logs. To do this, open SQL Server Management Studio, connect to SQL Server, and select the database of the report server. Then, right-click on it and choose **Properties**. Select **Options** on the left and then change the drop-down recovery model from full to simple and click on **OK**.

Reporting best practices

These are some of the SSRS best practices:

- Create a SQL Server scheduled task to automate the backup of the `ReportServer` and `ReportServerTempdb` databases
- Create a script to automate the backup of the key reporting service files
- Make a copy of the SSRS encryption keys to a safe location
- Make a copy of any custom SSRS reports
- Perform a script report backup with `RS.EXE`. For more information on `RS.EXE`, check out the following links:
  - http://msdn.microsoft.com/en-us/library/ms162839.aspx
  - http://msdn.microsoft.com/en-us/library/ms159720.aspx

Reports in the Configuration Manager console

The reporting section in Configuration Manager 2012 R2 can be found by navigating to **Monitoring** | **Overview** | **Reporting** | **Reports**. From the console, you can search and locate a specific report or a group of reports. If you want to find reports that contain software in them, enter `software` in the search field and click on **Search**. You can add additional search criteria by using the **Add Criteria** icon. You can run a report directly from the console. To do this, first select the report and click on the **Run** icon or right-click on it and choose **Run report**.

Creating a subscription

You need a report subscription in order to schedule report execution at a specific time, to be triggered by an event, and to post the results to a file share or even sent via e-mail.

You must enable these subscriptions on the reporting server in order to allow console settings to work. Open the Configuration Manager console and you can enable report subscriptions in two ways:

- From the menu, click on **Create Subscription**
- Choose a report, right-click on it, and then select **Create Subscription**

This will show you the **Subscriptions** tab from the report properties. Click on **Add** to add a new subscription. When you do this, the **Create Subscription Wizard** page starts. Enter the appropriate information and choose **Render Format** to design the report. Click on **Next** and enter the schedule information. You can also create and use the shared schedules. Click on **Next**. If the report has parameters, you can specify them as well. When the **Summary** page appears, review the information, and click on **Next** to save the subscription.

Managing SSRS report security

In order to manage report security from the SSRS report console, select **Report**, right-click on it, and choose **Properties**. After this, click on the **Security** tab. By default, the inheriting rights from the parent object are enabled. To modify them, disable the checkbox and click on the **Add** button for a set of roles to appear.

Creating a report

In order to create a report from the Configuration Manager console, you have to choose **Create Report** and launch the **Create Report Wizard** page. Then, you can choose to use a report model if it is present or a SQL-based report. For more information on report models, use the following link:

http://msdn.microsoft.com/en-us/library/ms345322.aspx

The next example uses a SQL-based report. You have to enter a name for the report and choose the path to select a folder location where you will save the report. Click on **Next** and review the **Summary** page. Click on **Next** again and then on **Finish** to deploy the report to the report server and to start Report Builder.

Creating custom reports

Sometimes, you need to create or modify an existing report in order to provide information that is not part of the core report. The following sections discuss development tools, how to create custom reports, interactive reporting features, and advanced reporting techniques so that you can create an advanced report.

Development tools

To create a custom report, you will need a development tool. The two primary tools to construct a custom report are Microsoft Report Builder and Microsoft Visual Studio:

- **Microsoft Report Builder**: Report Builder was first introduced in SQL Server 2005. Since then, Microsoft has released two upgrades. The newest version is SQL Report Builder 2012 R2. You can download it free from here:

  `http://www.microsoft.com/en-us/download/details.aspx?id=43346`

- **Microsoft Visual Studio**: This development tool has two components: Visual Studio Developer Edition and Business Intelligence Development Studio. You should consider Business Intelligence Development Studio as part of Microsoft Visual Studio, and because it is included with a SQL Server, no additional licensing is required. Business Intelligence Development Studio has the capability to create and maintain a whole custom reporting solution in one management window. A best practice is to use Report Builder 3.0 if you are a starter in this field.

Building a custom report

In this section, we will see how to create your own custom report. To create a report, you need to create a data source and define the data fields for your query.

The first thing you need is a data source. A data source can be created as a shared data source or it can be created to be used by the report. It is a best practice to create a shared data source because the data source can be secured and reused for multiple reports. Proceed with the following steps:

1. Go to the report server. The home page should be like that of `http://<reportserver>/reports`. You have to navigate one level down and reach the `Data Sources` folder. Then, click on **New Data Source**. You will see a window like the one in the following screenshot:

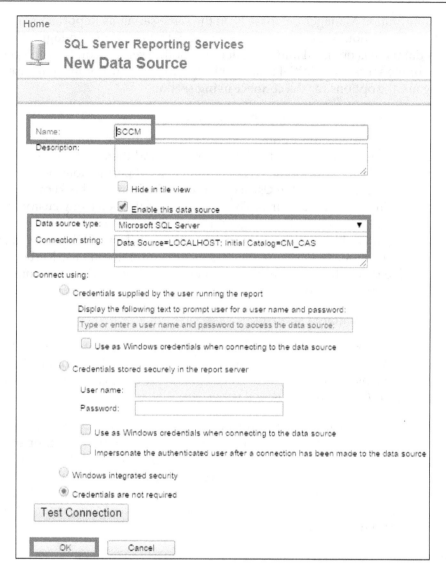

2. Next, you have to specify the settings for the data source. You have to provide a name, and the connection string will contain the necessary information to locate and communicate with the Configuration Manager database.

If the Configuration Manager database is on the same server as Report Server, the connection string should specify Data Source=LOCALHOST. If the Configuration Manager database is not local and is located on another server, you have to specify the name of the server. The initial catalog will specify the name of the database. The following are the options for the **connect-using** section:

- **Credentials stored securely in the report server**:

  If you want to use this option, you have to enter an account and password. This account and password will be encrypted and then stored on Report Server. This account should have a minimal set of permissions on the database server. Select the **Use as Windows Credentials** checkbox when connecting to the data source. This is very helpful when using custom report generation, because it allows a generic data source to be used instead of defining an individual user or group permissions. Here, SQL authentication is not recommended because it is less secure and it doesn't use Kerberos. The only scenario when SQL authentication is applicable is when you connect from an untrusted domain.

- **Windows integrated security**:

  This allows the current user to be authenticated on the database server. After you make your decision and select an option, click on **Test Connection** to check whether you can make a connection to the database. If it is successful, click on **OK** to save your new data source.

After the data source is defined, you must determine the data fields. In this example, we will create a report based on the number of computers based on their operating systems, and they will be displayed in a pie chart. Then, you must choose which data fields will be used in the query. If this is too complicated, you can always use SQL Server Management Studio. With it, you can view queries and see the results in the same windows and make quick adjustments. The SQL Server Management Studio platform is more powerful than Report Builder.

To create a chart, perform the following steps:

1. Open **Report Builder**, and on the first screen, select **Chart Wizard**:

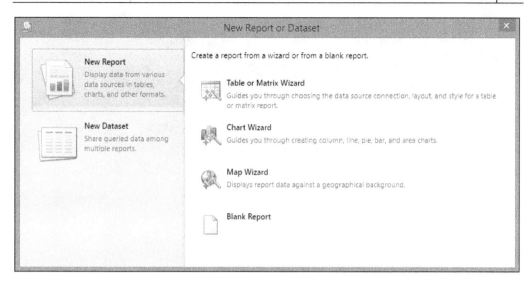

2. Select **Create a dataset** and click on **Next**:

3. On the data source properties window, click on **Build** to create a new data source, and you will see the following screenshot:

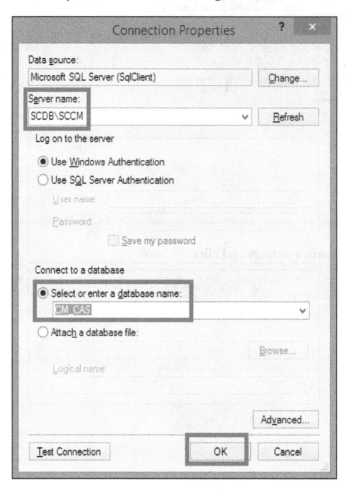

4. On the left-hand side of the **Design a query** page, you can see all the tables and stored procedures; when you select them, you will see the results on the right. Here, you can create the query as text if you click on **Edit as Text**:

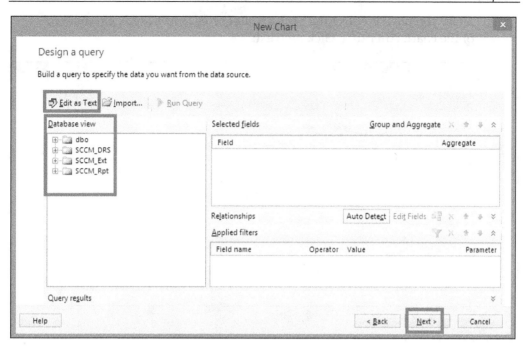

5. Click on **Next** and you reach the **Choose a chart type** page. Select the **Chart Type** option that suits your report the most:

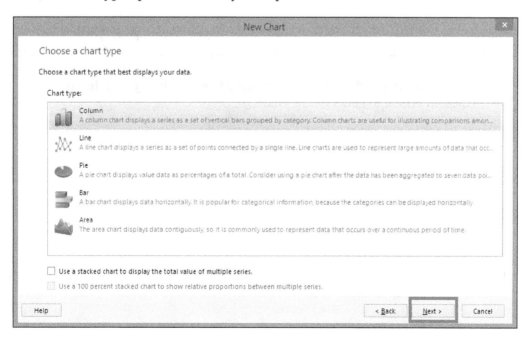

6. Next, you have to select the **Series**, **Categories**, and **Values** parameters of the chart. After that, click on **Next**:

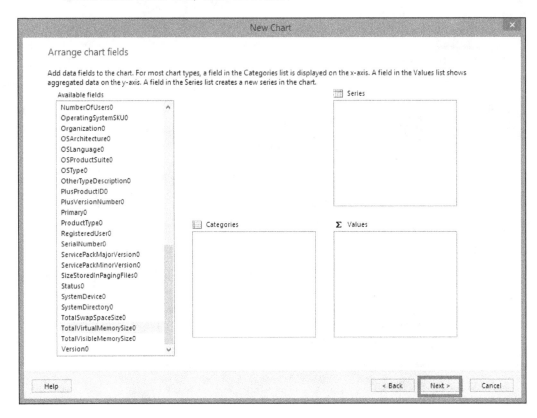

7. On the final page of the wizard, you have to select the style of the chart. Click on **Finish** to generate the chart:

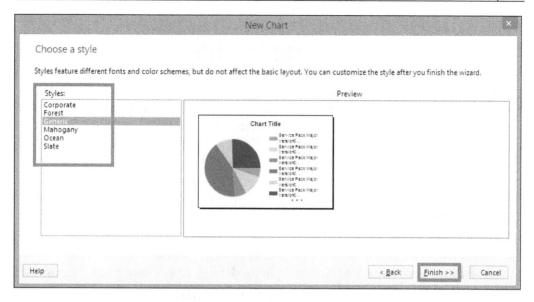

When you have finished creating the report, you can deploy it in Report Server. All reports are created in the XML format and are stored in a file type with the `.rdl` extension. Saving a copy of your custom report to a network share is always a good choice. After this, you have to upload the report to the report server. There are two ways to do this:

- From Report Builder, choose **Save As**, browse to Report Server, and save your new report.

- From Reporting Services, go to the **Custom Reports** folder and select the upload file and click on **OK**.

Report Builder is an excellent tool to browse, examine, and learn more about existing SSRS reports. For more information on Report Builder, go to:

`http://technet.microsoft.com/en-us/library/ee633667.aspx`

Interactive features of reporting services

These are the key interactive features of reporting services:

- **Report parameters**: Adding some parameters to the reports allows users to select specific values when the report is processed to filter the information represented in the report. This is accomplished by passing the selected parameter to the query used by the report. For example, you can provide a name of an update and filter all of the computer machines that have this update. Report parameters are very useful when making the report more flexible and versatile.

- **Interactive sorting**: This helps the user organize the data by any of the report columns.

- **Actions**: Reports can have links that will enable users to perform actions such as embedding links in a report to another piece of web content, drilling down to other reports for more details, and opening other reports.

- **Document maps**: A document map is used to navigate through a report easily. It is displayed in a side pane of the report. You can use it to move through different sections of the report.

- **Subreports**: Reports can be embedded inside another as a subreport. This enables developers to display information from one report as a subsection of another report.

Advanced custom report example

Now that we know how Reporting Services work and how they produce results, we can put them to use. The next example will be something from a life experience, something you can see in a real-world scenario: you need to apply security updates to your servers with the help of System Center Configuration Manager. Some of the servers have already been updated with these updates and the restart option is suppressed. The server restart is scheduled in 5 days' time. For this duration, servers will not have updates applied to them and they will be at risk. You have to check whether Configuration Manager administrators comply with the compliance settings and limit the report to only list servers and allow it to be flexible to check for reboots. In this example, we will need the following views from the Configuration Manager database:

`v_GS_COMPUTER_SYSTEM`, `v_GS_OPERATING_SYSTEM` and `v_GS_WORKSTATION_STATUS`.

Let's take a look at the SELECT statement:

```
SELECT
os.Caption0 as 'Operating System',
cs.Name0 as 'Server Name',
DateDiff(hour,os.LastBootUpTime0,ws.LastHWScan) as 'Uptime (in Hours)',
os.LastBootUpTime0 as 'Last Reboot Date',
ws.LastHWScan as 'Last Hardware Inventory'
FROM v_GS_COMPUTER_SYSTEM cs
INNER JOIN v_GS_Operating_System os
ON cs.ResourceID = os.ResourceID
LEFT OUTER JOIN v_GS_WORKSTATION_STATUS ws
ON ws.ResourceID = os.ResourceID
WHERE os.Caption0 LIKE '%server%'
AND ws.LastHWScan <> 0 AND cs.Name0 IS NOT NULL
```

The following is an explanation of the query:

- After the SELECT statement, there is a list of parameters that we will use in our final report
- You can give aliases to a certain parameter to make it more descriptive
- DateDiff is a SQL function that gives the difference between two dates
- We use the JOIN statements to bind information from multiple VIEW statements
- We also use alias names here to be more descriptive
- The final statement acts as a filter in order to limit the amount of information

Next, we have to create the report, and to do this, follow these steps:

1. Start Report Builder.
2. Click on **New Report** and select **Table** or **Matrix Wizard**.
3. Click on **Next** on **Shared Data Set Wizard**, select the shared **Data Source Connection** option, and then click on **Next**.
4. On the **Design a query** page, select **Edit as Text** and paste the query from before. Click on **Execute** in order to display the results.

5. Click on **Next**, and then in the arrange fields page, add the following:

   ◦ Server_Name

   ◦ Sum(Uptime_in_Hours)

   ◦ Last_Reboot_Data_Time

   ◦ Last_Hardware_Inventory

6. Continue clicking on **Next** until you click on **Finish**.

7. Next, you have to resize the columns and add a title to your report.

After the creation of the report, perform the following steps to customize it better:

1. You can add a report parameter to limit the data returned. To do this, go back to the **Design** view and right-click on **Parameter** and then select **New Parameter**. When the window appears, enter data for the following fields:

   ◦ **Name**: This is the name of the parameter

   ◦ **Prompt**: This is the value that will be entered

   ◦ **Data Type**: This is the data type of the prompt value

   ◦ **Select Parameter Visibility**: This determines whether the parameter is visible or not

2. If you want to display the servers that have not been restarted in 5 days, you need to change the default values on the **Parameter Properties** page. Navigate to **Default Values | Specify Values** and click on the **Fx** button on the right in order to start the **Expression Builder Wizard** page, which will help you create a custom function. Insert the following in the **Expression Builder** wizard:

   ```
   =DateAdd("d",-",-5, Now())
   ```

   This statement creates a date that is 5 days earlier than today. You can change this value as needed.

3. Click on **OK** twice to create this parameter.

The next step is to add this parameter to the report dataset. This will result in an interactive report that returns a list of servers that the last restart time was prior to the date specified in the parameter. In order to do this, follow these steps:

1. Start the **Report Builder** wizard and expand the **Datasets** node. Right-click on **Dataset1** and select **Dataset Properties**.

2. In the **Query View** page, enter the following statement right after the **WHERE** clause:

```
AND os.LastBootUpTime0 < @LastRebootDate
```

3. After this, you can add an interactive column sort that will allow users to sort the data and determine quickly which servers have not been restarted. Right-click on the **Uptime in Hours** column and select **Text Box Properties**. Choose **Interactive Sorting** on the left, select the **Enable interactive sorting** checkbox, and select the **Uptime in Hours** field that is located in the **Sort by** selection.

4. Save the changes by clicking on **OK**.

Save the report and give it a name, for example, `Server Restart Report`. When you run the report, it will display the servers that have a restart date less than the parameter value. Report users can enter a different date and make an interactive sort in the **Uptime in Hours** field. You can always export a specific report via e-mail.

Authoring best practices for report development

The following are the best practices regarding report development:

- The following suggestions are for dataset names:
  - Dataset names cannot contain spaces
  - Avoid changing the dataset name after you create it

- Enter a descriptive name that is different from Dataset1.
- Use Report Builder T-SQL Designer to create simple queries.
- Use SQL Server Management Studio Designer to build and test complex queries.
- Create queries based on Configuration Manager views because the views will work even after the product is upgraded. The database structure is different between Configuration Manager 2007 and 2012 versions and queries from 2007 might not work properly on a 2012 database.

 Microsoft doesn't publish the Configuration Manager database schema because it can change with another version. To avoid this impact, you should use database views.

- Also, avoid ORDER BY in the report query as you can use the sort sequence in the report dataset. This will reduce the overhead on the report server.

- Create and save custom reports on the SSRS server in a Custom Reports folder. This has several advantages:

  - It gives you the control to specify who has the ability to publish custom reports to SSRS

  - If you need to move a report to another SSRS server, you can find all reports in one folder

  - The report folder that is stored under the Configuration Manager folder is visible from the Configuration Manager console

Troubleshooting SSRS

SSRS doesn't need much troubleshooting after it is installed. Sometimes, you have to look for and resolve issues. There are two sections that you have to look at: log files and event-error logs.

SSRS logs

SQL Server Reporting Services utilizes a lot of log files that are generated by interaction with Configuration Manager and those native to SSRS. These are the sections that you should know about:

- SQL Server Report Server log files
- The Report Server Service trace log
- The Report Server execution log
- The Report Server HTTP log
- Srsrpsetup.log
- SrsrpMSI
- Srsrp.log
- The Windows authentication log

Optimizing SSRS performance

There are several SSRS features that can enhance report performance. They are subscriptions, report caching, report snapshots, and report timeout values.

Subscriptions

Subscriptions allow you to deliver a report to a server share on a scheduled basis. Enabling the report server's e-mail delivery gives you the ability to mail the contents of a report to an e-mail alias or deliver a copy of the report to a server share and a link to the report via e-mail. Subscriptions are valuable because you can schedule common report requests to be sent to users that need some information. You also have the additional advantage of scheduling complex reports to run in non-working hours.

Report caching

Report caching shortens the time for a user to retrieve a report, especially when the report is large. When a user sends a request for a report, a query is sent to the database. Then, an intermediate form of the report is cached on the report server and the final report is sent to the end user. This forces the intermediate form to be cached on the report server and provide users with more consistent user experience. Report caching is defined on a per-report basis. Open the Report Server, then select the **Manage Report** and **Cache Refresh** options to create and manage the cache plans.

Report snapshots

A report snapshot is a report captured at a point in time that contains all report content and results. They are run on a predefined schedule. They are presented in a format similar to HTML. This setting is per report. Go to **Report Manager**, select **Report Properties**, and then select **Report History**. For more information, check out this link:

```
http://msdn.microsoft.com/en-us/library/ms156291.aspx
```

Report timeout values

A very common issue with the Configuration Manager Legacy reporting was timeouts in the long-running reports or when reports returned too many rows. When using SSRS instead of ASP for reporting, it gives you the ability to configure report timeout values. In order to modify this setting, navigate to **Report Manager** and then **Site Settings**. The default setting is 1800 seconds, and you can change it. The change is made on a per-report basis. You can do this by navigating to **Report Manager** | **Report Properties** and selecting **Processing Options**. For more information on report timeout values, see this link:

```
http://msdn.microsoft.com/en-us/library/ms155782.aspx
```

Best practices for performance

Every report should begin with a properly designed query. When a report runs slowly, the first thing you have to do is take a look at the query. In some cases, you will not be able to modify the query so that it can perform faster. If this is the case, you can use report caching and report snapshots.

System Center Data warehouse

Microsoft System Center Service Manager 2012 implements a data warehouse to allow consolidation and reporting capabilities for the System Center suite. This also includes incident and change management created through Service Manager, Operation Manager Data, and the Configuration Manager hardware and software inventory that is imported into Service Manager with the help of a connector. The data warehouse uses a SQL Server database and a Service Manager Configuration Management database to store information, and also analysis services to present the data in a component called cube. An analysis services cube enables business and technical people to analyze the information by providing results they need to make decisions. With System Center 2012, Service Manager extends this capability to include data from Configuration Manager into the data warehouse. This information together with other System Center data such as Service Manager Incidents and Operations Manager data allow the decision makers in the company to take a look at the events and trends in a way that was previously not available. A connector between Configuration Manager and Service Manager feeds data from Configuration Manager to the Service Manager database, which is then presented via the data warehouse. Configuration Manager's data elements are as follows:

- Computers
- Hardware on computers
- Software on computers
- Software updates on computers
- Correlate DCM error events to incidents
- Mobile devices
- Power data
- Software update compliance data

Summary

SQL Server Reporting Services gives you the opportunity to show information contained in the Configuration Manager database using SSRS Reporting. It provides the security needed to manage the reports, and it also allows you to designate who can run and publish reports to the report server. SQL Server Management Studio, together with the Configuration Manager database, can be used to build queries prior to creating reports. Report Builder and Business Intelligence Development Studio can give the developer the tools needed to produce professional and versatile reports. SSRS also provides the additional functionality to fine-tune reports for performance and schedule them for an e-mail delivery. You can use the information contained in the reporting server database to understand which reports are candidates for performance enhancement and how reports are being executed in the environment. In the next chapter, we will take a look at the **Administration** section of the Configuration Manager console as well as how to monitor Configuration Manager.

Administration and Monitoring

5

This chapter lets you take a look at the different administration techniques in System Center Configuration Manager 2012 R2. It explains how to plan and design your Configuration Manager infrastructure in terms of sites and site planning, the different types of sites, and how to combine them. Then, it covers the role-based administration capabilities of System Center Configuration Manager 2012 R2; it also covers how to define different user roles and how to assign users to these roles so that you have restricted access to your Configuration Manager infrastructure. What follows next is alerting and how to configure and subscribe to alerts. This means that you can define your custom alerts so that you are notified of the occurrence of some events in the infrastructure. The chapter ends with a detailed explanation of the client settings.

The Configuration Manager's discovery methods

Making an inventory of all the available resources in your infrastructure is of great benefit. System Center Configuration Manager can use different discovery methods to find these resources. There are seven types of discovery methods in the Configuration Manager, as follows:

- **Active Directory Forest**: This method is used to discover entire Active Directory forests.

- **Active Directory Security Group**: This method is used to discover the Active Directory security groups in an Active Directory domain.

- **Active Directory System**: This method is used to discover the computer accounts in an Active Directory domain.

- **Active Directory System Group**: This method is used to discover a group of computer or user accounts in an Active Directory domain.

- **Active Directory User**: This method is used to discover the user accounts in an Active Directory domain.

- **Heartbeat**: This method is used by active Configuration Manager clients to update their discovery records in the database. Because it is initiated by an active client, heartbeat discovery does not discover new resources.

- **Network**: This method searches your network infrastructures for network devices that have an IP address. This allows you to discover devices that might not be found by other discovery methods, including printers, routers, and bridges.

The Active Directory forest discovery is a new method in System Center Configuration Manager 2012 R2, and it is used to discover trusted and untrusted forests, Active Directory sites, and IP subnets. This method can automatically create Active Directory site boundaries and IP subnet boundaries as they get discovered.

Hierarchy planning

You must have a good understanding of the objectives and need to set your goals, that is, the most important thing before you start designing a Configuration Manager hierarchy. A hierarchy can consist of a single standalone primary site, a single primary site with child secondary sites, or multiple primary sites connected by a **Central Administration Site (CAS)**. A primary site cannot be joined as the child of a primary site. Configuration Manager allows you to change your hierarchy by connecting a standalone primary site to a CAS or to add secondary sites as child nodes to a primary site.

Sites within a hierarchy will share replicated data, security policies, and different types of objects, such as software libraries, boundaries, and boundary groups. The top-level site in the hierarchy can be a single primary site or a central administration site. Some site server roles can provide services to the whole hierarchy, and some can provide services within a specific site. A Configuration Manager 2012 hierarchy cannot contain a Configuration Manager 2007 site, but you can have multiple hierarchies in the IT infrastructure, one that is of the 2007 version and another one of the 2012 version.

Configuration Manager sites

Every Configuration Manager system is part of a site. Every site has a site server, site database, and a three-character alphanumeric site code. This site code is unique in the hierarchy, the entire Active Directory forest, and all untrusted forests and domains, even across different versions and hierarchies of the Configuration Manager. There are three types of sites: central administration, primary, and secondary. When determining the site code, you should consider this:

- Check the following link for reserved names at `http://support.microsoft.com/kb/279868/en-us`.

- Avoid reusing site codes that have been previously used. A site code is stored in the site database. If you want to reuse a site code, you will see that all references from the old site are not removed, which can cause problems in your new Configuration Manager's infrastructure.

Central Administration Site

A central administration site is only needed when you have a large IT infrastructure and an infrastructure consisting of more than 100,000 devices. The central administration site will always be at the top of your hierarchy, meaning that it will be your top-level site. All the data replicated in the hierarchy will be visible from the CAS and that is why it is ideal for reporting. Also, reporting can be done on a standalone primary site. However, the best practice for a large infrastructure is to have the reporting configured on the CAS. A CAS is mandatory when you have multiple primary sites. The CAS doesn't support clients directly and system roles that provide services to clients. A CAS can only have primary sites as child sites.

Primary and secondary sites

Configuration Manager clients are always assigned to primary sites, and they receive policy updates from their assigned sites. Secondary sites are used at remote locations and they provide Configuration Manager services locally to the clients assigned to a primary site in the hierarchy. They cannot have clients assigned to them. Secondary sites can be administered from the parent primary site. System Center Configuration Manager requires that all sites have a site database and that they participate in the database replication. The central administration site and the primary site databases must be hosted on a full Microsoft SQL Server. A secondary site database can be hosted on a SQL Server Express or full Microsoft SQL Server. You can install the site database on a default or a named SQL Server instance.

Hierarchy-wide site system roles

Some site systems can provide services to the entire hierarchy. Some of these site system roles synchronize with Microsoft services. The following services should be configured in the top-level site in your hierarchy, which can be either the CAS or the standalone primary site:

- **The asset intelligence synchronization point**: This site role allows you to request on-demand catalog synchronization.

- **The top-level software update point**: Additional software update points are required at child primary sites that use software updates. These are optional at secondary sites.

- **The Endpoint Protection point**: Configuration Manager uses this role to accept System Center Endpoint Protection license terms and to set up the membership for Microsoft Active Protection Service. This role should be assigned to a server with a good Internet connection.

- **Certificate Registration Point**: Certificate profiles in System Center Configuration Manager R2 work with Active Directory Certificate Services and Network Device Enrollment Service roles to provision authentication certificates for managed devices in order to provide access to users to company data in a secure manner. For example, you can provide certificates for VPN access or Wi-Fi connections.

The following are site roles that can be deployed on multiple primary sites in the Configuration Manager hierarchy:

- **Application Catalog web service point**: This role gives data to the application catalog website point.

- **Application Catalog website point**: This role provides users with access to the software in the application catalog. This is why this role should be on a server on a high bandwidth network.

- **Distribution point**: This role distributes deployments to clients.

- **Fallback status point**: This is a role that should be on a server at a location that is reachable to clients when the management point is unreachable.

- **Management point**: This is a site system role that replies to the Configuration Manager clients' requests and accepts management data from Configuration Manager clients.

- **Enrollment point**: This is a site system role that enables enrollment for mobile devices and AMT functionality.

- **Enrollment proxy point**: This site system role communicates with mobile devices during their enrollment.

- **Out-of-band service point**: This is a site system role that provisions and configures Intel AMT-based computers for out-of-band management.

- **Reporting services point**: This role is used in the top-level site, where all the replicated data in the hierarchy is available for reports.

- **Software update point**: This is a site system role that runs Microsoft Widows server update services and allows Configuration Manager to use the WSUS catalog to scan Configuration Manager clients for software updates.

- **State migration point**: This is a site system role that stores the user state and settings migrated during the operating system's deployment.

- **System health validator point**: This is the Network Access Protection role.

The following roles are hierarchy-wide and can be deployed on CAS and additional sites:

- **System health validator point**: This is the Network Access Protection role

- **Reporting services point**: This role is used in the top-level site where all replicated data in the hierarchy is available for reports

Planning your hierarchy structure

The new content distribution functionality in Configuration Manager 2012 gives you the ability to span a single site across multiple geographical locations using WAN links more efficiently. A well-designed System Center Configuration Manager hierarchy is more likely to contain fewer, flatter, simpler, and easier ways to manage sites. The top site can be a single primary site or a CAS. A primary site cannot have another primary site as a child site. If you want to extend your Configuration Manager hierarchy with a primary site, you need to create a CAS. The reasons to create additional sites are given as follows:

- Exceeding the number of clients that a single primary site can handle

- An additional primary site distributes the load and reduces the impact of a primary site failure

- You might create an additional site to support Internet-based clients

- Locations that use different language versions of the Configuration Manager client and system software

- You might choose to install a primary or secondary site to manage content distribution across WAN links

The System Center Configuration Manager 2012 distribution point provides functionalities for managing networks more efficiently, which reduces the need for a secondary site.

Planning boundaries and boundary groups

System Center Configuration Manager 2012 R2 boundaries can define network locations in which client systems might reside. Boundaries are defined at the hierarchy level and are no longer used to define sites. They are used to control which distribution point is to be used by clients. Boundary groups can aggregate boundaries for efficient management. Boundaries have two functions, as follows:

- **Automatic site assignment**: In order to use this function, you have to configure one or more boundary groups for automatic site assignment. When automatic site assignment is in order, the client determines whether the current network location corresponds to a boundary group that is configured for site assignment. If the client is within a boundary, it will be assigned with the appropriate site. If you have a standalone site, automatic site assignment is not needed.

- **Preferred site systems**: Preferred site systems are distribution points or state migration points that can be associated with boundary groups. The clients in a boundary group that is associated with a protected site system use the system as a content source. In System Center Configuration Manager 2012 R2, preferred distribution points are configured by default.

Boundaries must be added to a boundary group in order to be used. Site assignment and content locations are configured on boundary groups instead of boundaries. In the same way, preferred site systems are associated with boundary groups. This is how boundaries are defined:

- Active Directory site
- IP subnet
- IP range
- IPv6 prefix
- A combination of the preceding objects

Preferred AD site and IP subnet boundaries don't work well with **Classless Inter-Domain Routing (CIDR)**. Classless Inter-Domain Routing uses a variable length of the subnet mask to provide more flexible addressing. Both the Active Directory site and the IP subnet boundaries use a specific subnet mask based on the legacy assignment of the specified subnet. When you are using these types of boundaries, you might face these problems:

Actual IP range or IP address	How Configuration Manager calculates the subnet
192.168.1.0 – 192.168.2.255 or 192.168.1.0/23	192.168.1.0
192.168.2.27/24	192.168.2.0/24

You can find out more about when to use IP address ranges as site boundaries at `http://blogs.technet.com/b/configmgrteam/archive/2013/03/01/when-not-to-use-ip-address-ranges-as-boundaries-in-configuration-manager.aspx`.

Although the client's IP address is within the range, the subnet mask IDs will not match and the client will not be assigned during discovery. In addition, clients such as workgroup clients are unable to retrieve site information from the Active Directory, or clients from an untrusted domain that don't have a trust relationship cannot use Active Directory sites as boundaries. For this reason, IP ranges or IPv6 prefixes are more suitable for boundaries.

In Configuration Manager 2007, Active Directory site boundaries were used to avoid the duplicate effort of subnet information maintenance in Active Directory and Configuration Manager. The new Active Directory forest discovery method in System Center Configuration Manager 2012 allows you to import subnet information from the Active Directory and create boundaries based on the IP address ranges automatically. If this is used in on a large scale, it can lead to performance issues.

Boundary groups are also used with content distribution to control the distribution points, that is, which clients across different locations will retrieve content. Because boundaries are hierarchy-wide, the boundary groups for content location are independent of sites and a distribution point can be shared between sites, but it cannot be a member of two different sites. This is useful for optimizing content delivery with network considerations. When a client is not in the boundary of a distribution point, they will use the deployment option you specify for slow networks. For different deployment types, there are different behavior types located in:

- On the **Content** tab of application deployment types

- On the **Distribution Points** tab of a package deployment

- On the **Download Settings** tab of a software update deployment

Overlapping boundaries are still not supported for automatic site assignment. If you use boundaries for automatic assignment, it is important to plan and maintain boundaries that suit the most and that don't overlap between them. Automatic site assignment can have unexpected results when a client is located at two different boundaries. Overlapping boundaries are supported for content distribution. For the clients that belong to two different boundaries, Configuration Manager will return all the distribution points associated with all the client-assigned boundary groups. The client will follow the normal distribution point location rules to select the distribution point from the list.

Client discovery and installation methods

System Center Configuration Manager manages a client system by installing a client on it. This topic will introduce some information regarding the planning for client discovery. These are the methods you can use to install the Configuration Manager client agent on a target system:

- **Client push installation**: This happens when the site server makes a connection to a potential client and starts the client installation process. Client installation requires a discovery of the system first. This is only required for automatic and manual client pushes using the console. You can set up a client push installation on a site-wide basis, or you can push the client to individual systems and collections. A client push installation has multiple dependencies that you have to configure, and you are also limited to setting up installation properties on a site-wide basis. This functionality allows you to control everything from the Configuration Manager console, which simplifies the administration. A client push also requires firewall exceptions on the client side and administrative rights. In terms of security, it is less secure.

- **Software update point based installation**: This method uses the existing software update infrastructure to install the client. A software update point based installation doesn't require the discovery of the system. If you are using Windows Server Update Services for software update deployment, you can use this method.

- **Manual installation**: This happens when the administrator logs on to the system and starts the CCMSetup client installation program manually. This method also doesn't require the discovery of the system. Manual installation has fewer dependencies, and it is perfect for testing purposes, but it doesn't scale well.

- **Logon script installation**: This is the same as manual installation but here a script that is executed on logon initiates CCMSetup. This method provides a high degree of control over the installation process. With this method, you have to plan and avoid excessive network traffic. In the Active Directory domain, you can maintain logon scripts from a central location and assign them with a group policy.

- **Group policy installation**: This method uses policy software assignment to execute the Windows Installer package for the client. It has full control over the installation process and little control over when the installation is performed; you have to plan carefully and avoid excessive network traffic. It is important to note that you cannot use a group policy for workgroup systems.

- **Upgrade installation**: This method uses the existing software distribution infrastructure to upgrade the client. The upgrade installation method requires discovery of the system.

System Center Configuration Manager uses the following methods for discovery:

- **Active Directory system discovery**: This method uses a Lightweight Directory Access Protocol query to retrieve information from the Domain Controller about the computers in that domain. If you use Active Directory system discovery, ensure that the Active Directory database is maintained and obsolete computer accounts are removed regularly. System discovery provides filters so that stale Active Directory objects are not discovered.

- **Active Directory group discovery**: This can also be used to discover computer accounts.

- **Network discovery**: This method uses network protocols to enumerate IP subnets and hosts.

You can configure each of the discovery methods at one or more sites in the hierarchy. Avoid that the same Active Directory object is discovered multiple times. When an object is discovered, the specific discovery method creates a **Data Discovery Record (DDR)**. This record is stored in the database and is replicated in the hierarchy. Active Directory system discovery provides an excellent way to discover computers in an Active Directory domain. A downside of this method is that Configuration Manager generates discovery records for old computer accounts that do not exist in the infrastructure anymore. To address this issue, Configuration Manager 2012 provides new Active Directory system discovery options that give you the ability to discover computers that have logged on to a domain in a given timeframe or a computer account that has its computer account password updated in a given timeframe.

Network discovery has the advantage of discovering potential client systems that are no longer a part or have never been a part of the Active Directory domain. Network discovery can also retrieve information about the network. You must configure Network discovery carefully in order to avoid excessive network traffic.

System Center Configuration Manager 2012 provides additional Active Directory discovery methods that retrieve information about the users, computers, groups, and the environment. Here are the discovery methods that you can choose from:

- Active Directory forest discovery retrieves information about Active Directory sites and IP ranges and creates these objects to define boundaries. This method requires network connectivity and access permissions to a Domain Controller.
- Active Directory group discovery retrieves information about security groups and distribution groups and enumerates them.
- Active Directory user discovery retrieves information about the Active Directory users.

If you use any of the Active Directory discovery methods, you have to execute them on a single site with the best connectivity to a Domain Controller. Choose the least heavily loaded site server and Domain Controller that meet this requirement. Avoid Active Directory discovery when the Domain Controller is under a heavy load.

You can also configure the Active Directory user discovery and Active Directory system discovery methods to discover any Active Directory attributes of the discovered objects.

Role-based administration

The Configuration Manager console is context-sensitive based on the security of the administrative users. The console will display only what the user can manage.

The **Show Me** concept in the System Center Configuration Manager 2012 console displays only the relevant workspaces, panes, nodes, and objects that the user can manage. By reducing the information in the console, navigation is easier.

The console is designed to reflect only what the user is assigned to do. This behavior means that specialized console customization is no longer required, because it will change and display what is allowed. This means that you deploy a single console and let the security details do the rest.

For the administrative user to use the Configuration Manager console, the user must be assigned to at least one role or the console will fail to connect to the server. After the role is defined when you start the Configuration Manager console, the objects that fall under the management scope of the user are displayed and are accessible. Everything else is hidden. The console will display content based on the assigned roles, scopes, and collections:

- **Roles**: These are visible resources such as workspaces, objects, nodes, and actions that are available by the administrative user's associated role

- **Scopes**: Only the objects that are associated with the assigned scopes can be managed

- **Collections**: Only the collections that are assigned and the collections that are child objects to them might be managed

Objects in the console exist in three states: shown, hidden, and disabled. For objects that are in the shown state, it is obvious that they are being displayed in the console. If the user has the permission to manage the objects, they are displayed in the console. If the object is a node, the parent objects are also displayed. Objects are hidden by default. You can make objects appear by granting access. Hidden behavior is determined by:

- **Actions**: If an administrative user does not have permissions to perform an action

- **Objects**: If an object does not belong to a security scope assigned to the administrative user

- **Nodes**: The node will not be displayed if you don't have permissions to access them

- **Workspaces**: If the workspace doesn't have at least one node, it will not be displayed

Objects that are disabled are displayed, but they are greyed out in the console and do not allow interaction. This is a typical scenario where the user is given only read permissions to the object.

In-console alerts

Alerts are new in Configuration Manager. When compared to status messages, alerts can provide more features and improvements. For example, alerts are state-based, meaning that they execute immediately as the condition changes and they provide a near real-time monitoring experience and subscription. Alerts in Configuration Manager are limited in functionality and should not be considered as a monitoring solution. If you need monitoring tools, use System Center Operations Manager, which is an enterprise-level alerting, notification, and performance metric tool.

Alerts are located in the monitoring workspace of the Configuration Manager console. The overview node provides a list of the recent alerts. Clicking on the **Alerts** node will display the list of available alerts in the **List** pane and give details about the selected alert in the **Details** pane.

Alerts are displayed in the following five states:

- **Active**: This is displayed when a condition is met
- **Cancelled**: This is displayed when a condition is no longer met
- **Disabled**: This is displayed when the alert is disabled
- **Never triggered**: This is displayed when the alert is created but no condition has been met yet
- **Postponed**: This is the same as **Disabled** with an expiration period to revert to the active state

Managing alerts

Alerts in Configuration Manager 2012 have a variety of actions. Actions are dependent on the state of the alert. These are the available alert actions:

- **Postpone**: Postponing an alert essentially ignores the alert for a specified period of time. When the period expires, the alert updates to the current state. Only active alerts can be postponed.
- **Edit comments**: You can add and edit comments on the alert to provide additional information.
- **Configure**: This action provides an alert with the ability to change the name, severity, and definition.
- **Enable**: This enables the selected alert.
- **Disable**: This disables the selected alert.
- **Refresh**: This action refreshes the entire list of alerts.
- **Delete**: Deleting an alert will remove it from the **Alerts** node and the list of recent alerts.

Configuring alerts

Viewing alerts is very easy because they are located in only one section of the Configuration Manager console. Configuring alerts is more complicated because alert configuration options are scattered across the console. Each alert configuration is different, but all in all, it uses the same basis. An alert configuration requires an alert to be enabled and to have a threshold value. The following table displays the location and function of the alerts:

Site server alerts	• Deployments • Database replication • Database drive capacity • Low side-loading activations (Windows 8)
Site system alerts	• Software update point • Management point
Client health alerts	• Client checks whether the pass or no results for active client fall below the threshold • Client remediation success rate falls below the threshold • Client activity falls below the threshold
Endpoint Protection alerts	• When malware is found • The same type of malware is detected on multiple computers • The same type of malware is repeatedly detected within the specified interval on a computer • Multiple types of malware is detected on one computer in a specified time interval

Subscribing to alerts

Alert subscription refers to malware alerts. This alert subscription sends an e-mail when malware is detected. The following is an example of how to set up a subscription for System Center Endpoint Protection:

1. Go to the **Monitoring** workspace, expand the **Alerts** node, and select **Subscriptions**.

2. From the ribbon, select **Create Subscription**.

3. When the **New Subscription** window opens, enter a name for the subscription.

4. You have to specify an e-mail address for the alert recipient. You can enter multiple recipients and separate them with a semicolon.

5. Select the e-mail language.

6. Finally, select the appropriate alerts and click on **OK**.

Client settings

Client settings are centrally defined settings, accessible through the Configuration Manager console. To see the client settings, you have to go to the **Administration** workspace. These settings allow a Configuration Manager administrator to control the behavior and all the functionalities of the client. System Center Configuration Manager 2012 allows you to specify client settings at a collection level, allowing you to define different settings as necessary. This is very helpful, but it can cause problems when a client belongs to multiple device collections and all of them contain different client settings. Starting with Configuration Manager 2012 R2, some new settings have been included, called Resultant Client Settings. This works the same way as GPResult does for group policies. To read more about Resultant Client settings and how to configure them, go to `http://technet.microsoft.com/en-us/library/gg682109.aspx`.

To resolve this, Configuration Manager lets you enter priorities and show the resultant client settings. The client settings with the highest priority win over the client settings with the lower priority. You have to design the priorities carefully in order to maintain consistent client behavior. This change also benefits Virtual Desktop Environment scenarios. Each Configuration Manager client randomizes the scheduled times for hardware inventory, software inventory, software update scans, software update deployment, compliance settings, and Endpoint Protection scans on virtual machines that are running on the same physical host. It also makes sure that the management point server does not hit all the clients at the same time.

Every Configuration Manager installation comes with default settings. These default client settings are configured at the hierarchy level and are applicable to all users and devices with or without custom settings. You can apply custom settings and override the default settings. The default client settings have a priority of 10,000 so that you can define 9,999 custom client device settings. When you create custom client settings, keep them to a minimum configuration and enter meaningful names.

To configure the default settings, select the **Administration** workspace and go to the **Client Settings** node. Then, open **Default Settings** by double-clicking on it or select **Properties** by right-clicking on the context menu or ribbon bar.

The following are some settings that will allow you to specify a simple or custom schedule:

- **Simple schedule**: This allows you to specify the action that will run regularly. The client determines when to run the action based on its installation date and distributes the load on the Configuration Manager infrastructure. This is a preferred option when the clients are **Virtual Desktop Infrastructure** (**VDI**) clients, because it minimizes the load on the physical host as not all the VMs run the same client action at the same time.

- **Custom schedule**: With this, you can specify the exact time to start the action. This means that each client receiving the schedule initiates the defined action at the same time. This might cause a high overhead on the Configuration Manager infrastructure. Consider a custom schedule where you have a process that runs at specific intervals and requires current information.

Defining a priority

Defining a priority allows you to specify which settings should be applied when a client receives multiple custom device or user settings. Settings with a lower priority take precedence over the settings with a higher priority. Default client settings have a priority of 10,000, so this means that any custom settings will always take precedence over the default settings. Custom settings are used when you want to provide specific settings that are applied to members of one or more collections. As an example, define a hardware inventory schedule for specific servers that are managed with Configuration Manager. The first custom client setting that is created receives a priority of 1, the second receives a priority of 2, and so on. You can later adjust the priority of the custom client settings by right-clicking on the context menu or using the buttons from the ribbon bar.

Custom client settings might be deployed to multiple collections. Select the setting, choose **Deploy** from the ribbon bar, and then select the collection. Keep in mind that custom client device settings can be deployed only to device collections, and custom client user settings can be deployed only to user collections.

Background Intelligent Transfer Service device settings

The **Background Intelligent Transfer Service (BITS)** device settings allow you to configure the behavior of BITS. BITS provides bandwidth control over the transfer or provide packets on the network between Configuration Manager clients and their management points. It is also used to download content from the distribution point. If you enable BITS, there are several options to control its behavior. One of them is to use start and stop times for a throttling window, allowing BITS downloads outside a defined control window and a transfer rate during and outside the window. Before going further, you have to set BITS bandwidth limitations. To do this, follow these steps:

1. Log on to the computer with an account that is a member of the local administrators group.

2. Click on the Start icon, click on **Run**, type `gpedit.msc`, and then press *Enter*.

3. In the pane on the left-hand side of the **Group Policy Management Console (GPMC)**, expand **Computer Configuration**, **Administrative Templates**, **Network**, and then click on **Background Intelligent Transfer Service**.

4. In the **Setting** pane, double-click on **Limit the maximum network bandwidth for BITS background transfers**.

5. In the pane at the top of the dialog box, click on **Enabled**.

6. In the **Options** pane, set the transfer rate in kilobits per second (Kbps) that you want BITS to use. The default value is `10` Kbps.

7. Set the time during which you want to limit the bandwidth. The default setting is from 12:00 A.M. to 12:00 A.M.

8. Specify the bandwidth limitations to use outside the designated time. The default setting is **Use all available unused bandwidth**.

9. Click on **OK** to finish.

After you finish configuring BITS with the **Limit the maximum network bandwidth for BITS background transfers** option, you can modify the following settings:

- Specify the timeframe to enable the BITS bandwidth control by entering a start and stop time

- If the bandwidth control should always be enabled, set the start and stop time for bandwidth control to the same value

- Specify the maximum transfer rate during the control windows in Kbps
- Specify whether you use using bandwidth control outside of the specified control window by entering a maximum transfer rate in Kbps

If you configure BITS settings using a group policy, the GPO settings will overwrite the settings that come from Configuration Manager and the other way around, leading to unwanted results.

Client policy device settings

Client policy device settings define the interval at which you can download policies from the management point. By default, a client requests for a policy from its management point every 60 minutes. You can modify the policy refresh period to between 3 minutes and 1,440 minutes or 24 hours. An aggressive schedule can introduce a performance impact on clients and servers. When the **Enable user policy polling on clients** setting is **False**, users will not receive applications and the other operations contained in user policies. Users will not receive revisions and updates for the applications published in the application catalog and will also not see any notifications about their application approval requests. User policy requests from the Internet clients can work only when the **Enable user policy polling on clients** setting is **True** and the Internet-based management point can successfully authenticate the user using Windows Authentication.

Mobile device client settings

Beginning with System Center Configuration Manager 2012 R2, a new compliance settings option is added in the **Create Configuration Item Wizard** pane, which is found in the **Assets and Compliance** section of the Configuration Manager console. This new compliance setting allows you to configure the definition of a mobile device's client settings and settings group. This new compliance setting can be applied to the following mobile device platforms:

- Windows Mobile (support for Windows Mobile 6.1 and 6.5)
- Symbian Mobile (support for all Nokia Symbian devices)
- Windows Phone (support for all Windows Phones 8.0)
- Windows 8 (support for all Windows RT)
- Windows 8.1 (support for all Windows RT)
- iPhone (support for iOS 5, 6, and 7)
- iPad (support for iOS 5, 6, and 7)
- Android (support for Android 4.0, 4.1, and 4.2)

You can apply the following mobile device settings groups:

- Password (password length and expiration)
- Device (device restrictions to apply to mobile devices)
- E-mail management (typical settings for e-mails such as allowed protocols, attachments, and archives)
- Store (defines the settings for the application store on the device)
- Browser (specifies the default web browser settings)
- Internet Explorer (specifies settings for Internet Explorer on Windows-based mobile devices)
- Content rating (settings for content rating information for media and application)
- Cloud (settings for cloud restrictions to be applied to mobile devices)
- Security (typical security settings such as file signing, application, Bluetooth, and cameras)
- Peak synchronization (includes settings that control the hours and frequency of mobile device synchronization)
- Roaming (settings that configure download options for mobile devices when they are on roaming)
- Encryption (encryption settings for devices, e-mails, and storage cards)
- Wireless communication (settings that configure wireless connections for mobile devices)
- Certificates (specifies which certificates need to be installed on mobile devices)
- System security (typical settings for system security such as firewall, automatic updates, and virus protection)
- Windows server work folders (specifies typical windows server work folder settings)

Compliance settings for device settings

Using compliance settings for device settings, you can enable or disable the functionality they provide. Reporting and alerting on compliance helps to monitor and manage the configuration drift. You can apply compliance settings to desktops, servers, mobile devices, and users, and you can remediate Windows Management Instrumentation, registry, and script settings for noncompliant configurations. Automated remediation can drastically reduce the time for which a noncompliant configuration stays out of compliance.

Computer agent device settings

Computer agent device settings allow you to define settings related to software distribution on Configuration Manager clients. These include specifying the notification interval for deployments, the default Application Catalog website point, and more. What follows is information regarding the following settings:

- **Deployment deadline**: You can specify the notification intervals before a deployment deadline is reached:

    ○ Users, by default, are notified 48 hours in advance when the deployment deadline is greater than 24 hours, and you can modify the value from 1 to 999 hours.

    ○ If the deployment deadline is less than 24 hours but more than 1 hour, users are reminded every 4 hours. This setting can be modified between 1 and 24 hours.

    ○ If the deployment deadline is less than 1 hour, users are notified every 15 minutes. This setting can be modified between 5 and 25 minutes.

- **Application Catalog**: These settings are related to the default Application Catalog:

    ○ **Specifying the server that hosts the Application Catalog website**: It is recommended that you use the **Network Basic Input/Output System (NetBIOS)** name to prevent clients from receiving a prompt for credentials when connecting to the website. Specify the NetBIOS name on the website's point properties and use the name resolution mechanism.

    ○ **Use automatic detection to allow a client to receive the closest Application Catalog**: Automatic detection uses a service location request sent to a management point. This request occurs every 25 hours. After that, the management point returns the Application Catalog website depending on the location of the client. Automatic detection is useful because clients are pointed to an Application Catalog automatically, according to their site. Different Application Catalogs can be specified for clients that reside on the Internet and the intranet. The Application Catalog website uses HTTPS instead of HTTP. You might decide not to use automatic detection when you want to specify manually which clients connect to which server, and when you don't want to wait for 25 hours for website point changes.

    ○ Specifying a URL to a customized Application Catalog allows you to specify a URL to a custom website that hosts the Application Catalog.

      °   When the Application Catalog website is not added to the trusted zone in the Internet Explorer settings on the client site, Internet Explorer's protected mode will not allow you to install an application from the Application Catalog. If you have this scenario, just add the Application Catalog website to the list of trusted sites manually or through a group policy.

- **Configure install permissions**: Here, you specify which users can initiate software installations, software updates, and task sequences. This setting is set to **All Users** by default. If you set it to **No Users**, required deployments for the computer are always installed on the deployment deadline and users will not initiate software installation from the Software Center or Application Catalog. You can also enable this feature for **Administrators only** or **Administrators and Primary Users only**.

      °   **Agent extensions manage the deployment of application and software updates**: If you use a third-party solution of the software development kit or any third-party vendor that connects to a Configuration Manager server, you must set it to **True**

- **PowerShell**: If your clients run PowerShell 2.0 or higher, you can specify the PowerShell execution policy that identifies the execution policy to be used during Configuration Manager actions. By default, this setting is **Restricted** but if you set it to **Bypass** or **Unrestricted**, you can use unsigned scripts.

- **Notifications**: You can enable or disable notifications for new deployments by setting the **Show notification for new deployment** setting to **False** or **True**.

Computer restart device settings

Computer restart device settings allow you to enter the time frame when Configuration Manager will initiate a system restart:

- The display countdown interval setting before log off and restart is 90 minutes by default and can be set between 1 minute and 1,440 minutes

- The display countdown interval before final log off and restart in minutes is 15 minutes by default and can be set to any value between 1 minute and 1,440 minutes

You have to be certain that the intervals you specify are shorter in duration than the shortest maintenance windows so that the system can restart during that window.

Hardware inventory device settings

These settings allow you to enable or disable the hardware inventory and define its settings.

When hardware inventory is enabled, you can specify the schedule. By default, it is set to 7 days, but you can specify a custom schedule. You can specify how to collect management information files, identify a maximum file size, and define hardware inventory classes.

Configuration Manager 2012 simplifies the configuring and extending of the hardware inventory. You can set client settings in more detail, making it possible to define other hardware inventory settings for laptops, compared to traditional desktop systems. You have to configure the items you want to make an inventory of by modifying the settings for hardware inventory in the configuration of the default client settings. In order to do this, perform the following steps:

1. Go to the **Administration** section of the console and navigate to **Overview | Client Settings**.
2. Select **Default Client Settings** and choose **Properties**.
3. Select **Hardware inventory** and then click on the **Set Classes** button to open a new dialog window, where you can enter the inventory classes. The classes can be either enabled or disabled.

    ° If the class has a grey checkmark, the class and some of its properties are inventoried

    ° If the class is not checked, it is not inventoried

    ° If the class has a black checkmark, it means that not all properties are inventoried

You can modify the list by defining custom client device settings and allowing you to specify different selections for specific collections.

There are many ways to extend the inventoried items, as shown here:

- Import an MOF file using the import functionality, which allows you to browse for MOF files
- Export settings to an MOF file, which can be used later to import into another Configuration Manager infrastructure

MIF files are used when you want to extend the hardware inventory information. They can also be used to transport information that may not be available in the system. For example, you can write a tool that collects information from the end user and stores the output in the MIF format that can be picked up by the Configuration Manager inventory. The information stored in the MIF file is sent and stored in the site database. In order to learn how to create MIF files and extend your hardware inventory, follow the guidelines at `http://blogs.technet.com/b/configurationmgr/archive/2014/07/02/a-step-by-step-guide-to-configuring-noidmif-for-hardware-inventory-in-configuration-manager-2012.aspx`.

This means that the collected information is available with the default client inventory data. There are two types of MIF files, NOIDMIF and IDMIF files.

Data collected from NOIDMIF and IDMIF files is not validated. This means that data can be used to overwrite valid data that is stored in the database and can potentially break the functionality of the Configuration Manager site:

- **NOIDMIF**: These files are associated with the client on which the NOIDMIF file is inventoried. For Configuration Manager to process the NOIDMIF file, place it in the `%windir%\CCM\inventory\noidmifs` folder.

- **IDMIF**: These files are associated with the client they are collected from, allowing you to collect the inventory about non-Configuration Manager client devices. IDMIF files are collected only if they meet the maximum custom MIF file site, which is 250 KB by default. These files should be stored in the `%windir%\CCM\inventory\idmifs` folder to be picked up by Configuration Manager hardware inventory.

You can modify the MIF storage locations in the registry by modifying the registry key that specifies the location of both the files. The registry key is located under `HKLM\Software\Microsoft\SMS\Client\Configuration\Client Properties` and can be specified by modifying the NOIDMIF directory and IDMIF directory values.

The configuration Manager client can scan the hardware currently installed on the client and report the information back to the Configuration Manager infrastructure. From the Configuration Manager console, a Configuration Manager user can start the Resource Explorer and view the inventoried hardware for a specific client. The inventory also takes the hardware changes into account and gives IT administrators the ability to determine whether there were hardware changes between inventories.

The hardware that is inventoried is defined centrally in the Configuration Manager settings, which might be changed to gather additional hardware or leave out specific hardware information. If the client is not connected to the network during the inventory process, the inventory takes place and data is uploaded when the connection is established again. If the client is offline during the inventory process, the process for that client will take place when the client is online.

Hardware inventory also inventories the software available through the **Programs and Features** applet from **Control Panel**. This determines the software installed on the client system. Not all software is advertised in the following registry key:

```
HKEY_LOCAL_MACHINE\SOFTWARE\Microsoft\Windows\CurrentVersion\
Uninstall
```

You will use the software inventory to get a full inventory of the client system's software and files that are found on the disk and match the configured rule. It gives more overhead to the client and the server and doesn't provide great value.

When the standard hardware inventory does not give you all the information, it can be because the new hardware is unknown to Configuration Manager. However, you can modify the Configuration Manager configuration to enable an inventory for extra hardware.

Network access protection device settings

The Configuration Manager client supports **Network Access Protection (NAP)** and can use Configuration Manager for remediation when systems are noncompliant. Compliance is determined by a System Health Validator Point. The Configuration Manager clients need to have the Network Access Protection Agent service started, and the backend infrastructure that supports NAP should be in place.

When the **Enable Network Access Protection on clients** setting is set to **True**, NAP will evaluate the clients that support the NAP infrastructure. When **Require a new scan for each evaluation** is set to **True**, a client will wait until scanning is completed to send its results for evaluation. This is the most secure setting, but it is the required time before the client is permitted on the LAN. If the setting is **False**, by default, the client receives the result of the latest evaluation, which reduces the time frame for the evaluation process.

Power management device settings

Power management settings specify whether the power management capabilities, for the client, by the Configuration Manager are enabled or disabled and if users can exclude the device from these settings.

Remote control device settings

The remote control settings specify whether the remote control on clients is enabled. You can also specify whether users will be allowed to change the remote control settings and notification settings in the Software Center client applet, whether the remote control of an unattended computer is permitted and whether to prompt the user for permission, and whether users that are local administrators on the client might use the remote control.

You can also configure the access level, which can be **Full Control**, **View Only**, and **No Access**. You can specify permitted viewers by listing the Active Directory group or an Active Directory user.

You can use remote tools for the remote management of client desktops for troubleshooting purposes, which is a common scenario. Using this functionality with Configuration Manager that is executed from a central point provides logging capabilities and the report functionality. Before you can use remote tools, you must prepare the clients by enabling the Remote Tools Client Agent. You can use remote tools in a couple of ways, either by completely taking over the desktop or assisting the end user using the Remote Assistance functionality.

Configuring remote control and remote assistance

Many organizations provide remote support for their end users. Windows OS includes several ways to provide support using Remote Desktop Session and Remote Assistance; many organizations require the remote control of workstations to be managed and logged from a central location.

The remote control depends on the effective default or custom client device settings on the Configuration Manager client. The remote tools' client settings allow you to enable remote control on clients. You can also edit the remote tools' client settings by navigating to **Administration | Overview | Client Settings** and selecting **Default Client Settings**, modifying custom device settings, and creating custom device settings. Open the **Remote tools** section and click on **Configure**. This will start the **Remote Control and Windows Firewall Client Settings** dialog box and enable the checkbox for **Enable Remote Control on client computers**. When enabled, there are other settings that you can configure:

- Specify whether Configuration Manager should configure the Windows firewall of the destination computer with rules to allow it to be remotely controlled.

- Specify whether users can modify the policy or notification settings in the Software Center. When this is enabled, the user can specify whether they want to use the remote access specified by the Configuration Manager administrator or whether they want to enter their own values.

- In the client settings, specify whether to enable the remote control of an unattended computer.

- Specify whether the user is prompted for remote control permissions so that if the user is logged on, they are presented with a dialog box requesting permission for remote control.

- Specify who can initiate remote control by configuring permissions and allowing members of the local administrators group or another Active Directory group or user.

- Specify the types of notifications that the users will receive when remote control is active.

- The remote tools' client settings also allow you to manage solicited and unsolicited remote assistance settings. When set to **True**, Configuration Manager manages remote assistance, where the user at the client computer requests or doesn't request assistance.

- When the **Manage Remote Desktop Settings** value is set to **True**, Configuration Manager manages the remote desktop settings of the client receiving the settings.

- The **Allow permitted viewers to connect by using Remote Desktop connections** setting allows users specified in the permitted viewers list to set up a remote connection.

- The **Require network level authentication on computers which run Windows Vista and later** setting configures the remote desktop connection to use NLA in order to connect to the remote computer.

Using a remote control

Remote control provided by System Center Configuration Manager gives the administrators the ability to watch a remote desktop session locally and to take control of the mouse and keyboard, and assist in the troubleshooting process or perform actions on the remote system. You can start the **Remote Control** viewer from the Windows Start menu or the Configuration Manager console. Configuration Manager also allows you to start a remote assistance or remote desktop session on the remote computer.

If the connection to the machine that is remotely controlled is lost, the remote computer is locked. Remote control now supports multiple monitors. The notification bar is visible on the remote computer and it displays the account name of the user that is controlling the computer. Remote control uses TCP port 2701 and RDP uses TCP port 3389. If Kerberos authentication fails when you want to take control over a computer, the system prompts if you want to use NTLM authentication.

Remotely administering a client computer

To remotely administer a target computer, you have to go the **Assets and Compliance** workspace and select the client computer from the **Devices** node. When selected, select **Start** and click on **Remote Control** to start the remote control viewer. The permissions that you set using the remote tools' client settings determine whether you can view or take full control over the remote machine.

You can also start the remote control viewer from the command line. The executable file is CmRcViewer.exe and is located in the <Configuration Manager Install Path> \ Admin Console\Bin\x64 folder. Supply the following two values when connecting to a client computer with this command-line utility:

- The NetBIOS name or the FQDN name of the client you want to administer remotely
- The site server you will send state messages to

Providing remote assistance

You can also start providing remote assistance to a client computer from the **Assets and Compliance** workspace by selecting the client computer from the **Devices** node and clicking on **Start** and then clicking on **Remote Assistance** to start the remote assistance client.

To use the remote assistance functionality, remote assistance must also be installed on the machine that is running the Configuration Manager console. You can use a remote desktop to connect to a client computer from the **Assets and Compliance** workspace if you select the client computer from the **Devices** node. Click on **Start** and then click on **Remote Desktop Client** to start an RDP session to the client.

Using remote control from Configuration Manager has a great advantage because remote control actions are audited by Configuration Manager and can be retrieved using two reports:

- All computers that are remote controlled by a specific user
- All remote control information

Software deployment device settings

These settings allow you to enter the time when software deployments are re-evaluated. Software deployment re-evaluation sets the schedule when clients re-evaluate the installation status of previous deployments and updates. If some updates or software deployments are missing, they are reinstalled from a local cache or downloaded from the distribution point. Selecting the schedule allows you to change the default value, if it is a custom schedule.

Software inventory device settings

The software inventory device settings allow you to enable or disable a software inventory.

Consider a software inventory as a file inventory. It enables you to inventory certain files based on predefined search parameters. This could be to inventory all the executables, which could complement the inventory information coming from the hardware inventory. When the software is inventoried, the information in the file header of the inventoried file is made available in the Configuration Manager console, and this allows the Configuration Manager administrator to report on the software inventory or use the information to create collections for software distribution. Software inventory does not include the deltas. It means that it only stores the latest data that is uploaded. The software inventory also lets you upload specified files to the Configuration Manager hierarchy. Inventorying all executables on a client is not a good practice. It is better to inventory only the %ProgramFiles% folder. For example, you can scan for some .txt files that match some criteria and upload them to the inventory.

To configure the software inventory, you have to do the following:

1. Go to the **Administration** workspace of the console and navigate to **Overview | Client Settings**. Select either **Default Client Settings** or **Custom Device Settings**. You can also create new custom device settings.

2. In the **Software Inventory** section of the device settings, configure the software inventory:

   ° Enable the software inventory by setting the **Enable software inventory on clients** value to **True** and specify a schedule when clients should execute the software inventory

   ° Setting inventory reporting details lets you specify what to report about the inventory

   ° Configure the types of files to inventory by clicking on the **Set Types** button as part of the **Inventory these file types which starts the Configure client settings** page

Using Resource Explorer

The Resource Explorer is executed from the Configuration Manager console. It provides an insight into the hardware and software inventory. To start the Resource Explorer, you have to do this:

1. Go to the **Assets and Compliance** section. Select **Devices** and locate the device.

2. Select the device for which you want to see information and navigate to **Start | Resource Explorer**.

The nodes shown by the Resource Explorer are:

- Hardware
- Hardware history
- Software

Summary

In this chapter, we learned about the way in which the System Center Configuration Manager hierarchy is organized. We discussed boundary groups, how to create them, and how to configure them. We also discussed primary and secondary sites as well as CAS as different types of sites that can be configured in the Configuration Manager infrastructure. After that, we talked about different ways to discover systems in the infrastructure. At the end, we discussed all the aspects of client settings and how to use these settings to make an optimal configuration for your business needs.

In the next chapter, we will take a look at Windows Intune and Windows Azure, how you can integrate your Configuration Manager infrastructure, and use the public cloud to add value to your Configuration Manager infrastructure.

6
Cloud Integration

System Center Configuration Manager 2012 R2 can use Microsoft's public cloud services in order to provide an even greater value to your organization. You can use Windows Azure as a backup location so that clients can access your services and applications. Another service that you can integrate with is Windows Intune. You can use Windows Intune together with System Center Configuration Manager to deliver applications to mobile devices, to manage them, and to provide them with secure access to your company data.

Cloud integration – prerequisites

In order to integrate Configuration Manager with the public cloud, you have to fulfil the prerequisites. The prerequisites can be classified into the following groups:

- **External dependencies**: These dependencies are external to System Center Configuration Manager 2012 R2

- **Obtain certificates or keys depending on the platform**: Depending on the mobile device platform, you need to import either certificates or side-loading keys in order to manage the platform

- **Internal dependencies**: These dependencies are internal and refer to the Configuration Manager

- **Prerequisites for mobile device enrollment**: These include other configurations, either internal or external to the Configuration Manager, that are needed for managing mobile devices

You can find more about them at `http://technet.microsoft.com/en-us/library/jj884158.aspx#bkmk_preq`.

Subscribing to Windows Intune

One of the prerequisites before you can start the integration of System Center Configuration Manager 2012 R2 and Windows Intune is to subscribe to the Windows Intune service. For the purpose of testing, you can create a 30-day trial of the Windows Intune subscription. To create a trial subscription, go to the following link and proceed with the instructions:

```
https://account.manage.microsoft.com/Signup/MainSignUp.
aspx?OfferId=A77BE827-FC8B-4EF2-A0F5-7CD6C813AA65&ali=1
```

After you have completed the sign up process and have logged in to your account, you will see a screen similar to the following screenshot:

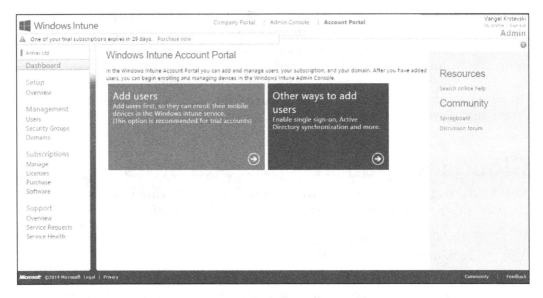

On the left-hand side of your web page, you can see all the menus, and at the top, you can see the **Company Portal** and **Admin Console** options. If you go to the **Users** menu, on the left, you will see a screen as shown in the following screenshot:

Set up and manage Active Directory synchronization

Synchronize your local Active Directory® and see your global address list in Windows Intune.

If you haven't done so already, we strongly recommend that you set up single sign-on to allow users to sign in to Windows Intune with their corporate credentials.

You only need to set up single sign-on, Active Directory synchronization, and a registered domain one time for a Microsoft Online service. If your company is already using Microsoft Office 365 or another Microsoft Online Service, then some or all of these setup steps may be complete. After you setup single sign-on, Active Directory synchronization, or a registered domain for Windows Intune, these items will be available for your other Microsoft Online services.

1   Prepare for directory synchronization
    Check prerequisites, including computer requirements and user permissions.
    Read: Prepare for directory synchronization

2   Verify domains
    For a better user experience, go to the domains page to add and verify your company's
    domains before you continue with the steps on this page.

3   Activate Active Directory synchronization
    Activate directory synchronization to use your local Active Directory to add or remove
    users and security groups and sync to Windows Intune. After you activate directory
    synchronization, you cannot deactivate it. Learn more

    [Activate]

4   Install and configure the Directory Synchronization tool
    Download the Directory Synchronization tool and then configure it to set up
    synchronization from Active Directory to Windows Intune.

In the **Users** menu, you can synchronize data between your on-premises Active Directory and Azure Active Directory. Furthermore, you can set up Single Sign On, which will enable users to use their company credentials.

Adding the Windows Intune subscription to Configuration Manager

The first thing you need to do before you can use Windows Intune is to create a Windows Intune subscription. To add a Windows Intune subscription to your Configuration Manager infrastructure, you have to perform the following steps:

1.   Go to the **Administration** section of the Configuration Manager console.

2. Expand **Cloud Services**, right-click on **Windows Intune Subscription**, and then click on **Add Windows Intune Subscription**, as shown here:

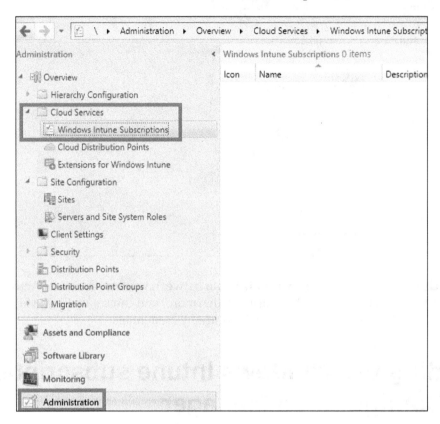

3. This will start the wizard; you can add the Windows Intune subscription and just click on **Next**, as shown in the next screenshot:

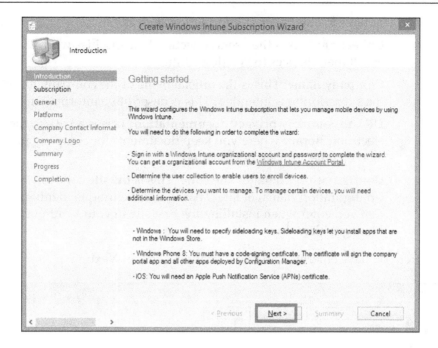

4. In the next window, you have to click on **Sign In** to enter your Windows Intune subscription's username and password, provided that you already have one. If you don't, you will have to create one. After your credentials are validated, click on **Next**, as shown here:

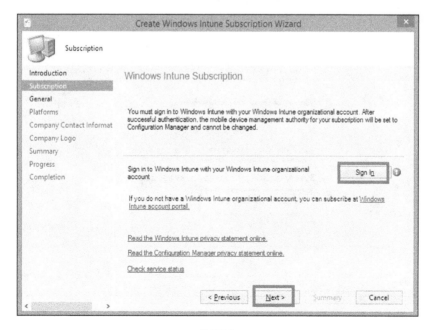

5. Here, you have to enter a lot of information such as:

    °   **Collection**: This is the users collection that specifies which users can enroll their devices to Windows Intune.

    °   **Company name**: This is the official name of the company for which the subscription is intended. This is descriptive information.

    °   **URL to company privacy documentation**: This is a URL to the electronic library where you keep documents for company privacy or keep other private documents.

    °   **Configuration Manager site code**: This is the site code of your Configuration Manager site. That is, it is the unique identifier that you enter when installing the first site in your Configuration Manager hierarchy.

6. After you have entered all the information, click on **Next**:

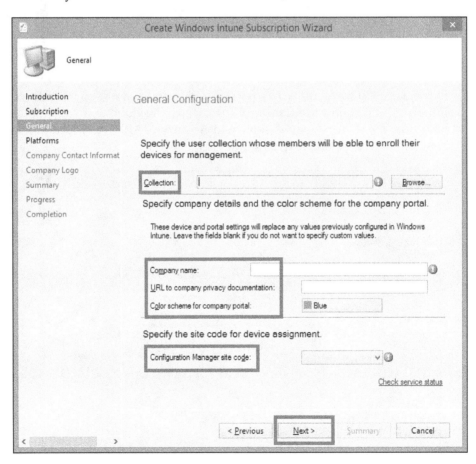

7. In this step, you can choose the device platforms that can be enrolled in Windows Intune. The available platforms are:

   ° **Android**

   ° **iOS**

   ° **Windows**

   ° **Windows Phone 8**

8. After you have selected all the platforms that you need, click on **Next**, as shown here:

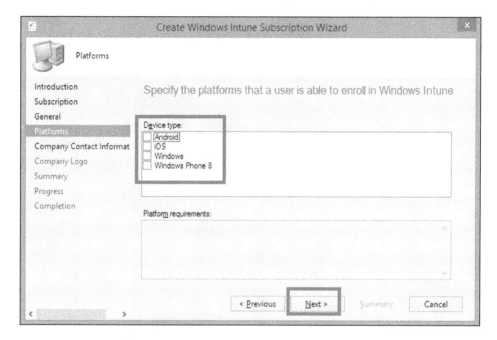

9. In this step, you have to enter all the requirements for the mobile platforms:

   ° For Windows, you have to enter the **Code-signing certificate** and **Sideloading keys** options, as shown in the following screenshot. There are three ways to obtain a code-signing certificate, as follows:

   ° Purchase a code-signing certificate from a commercial certificate vendor

   ° Create a code-signing certificate using Active Directory Certificate Services

   ° Create a code-signing certificate using MakeCert

○ You can find more details about the process of creating code-signing certificates at `http://technet.microsoft.com/en-us/library/cc732597(WS.10).aspx`.

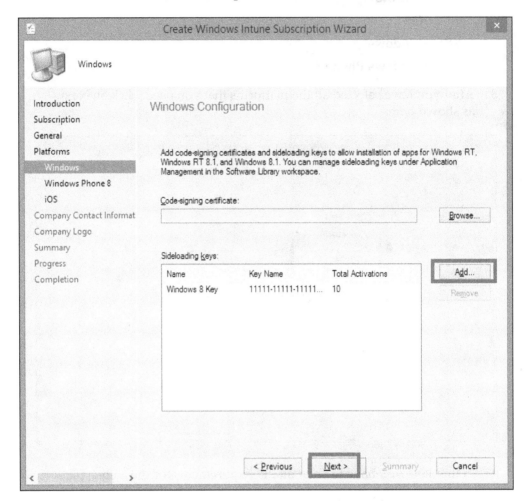

○ For Windows Phone 8, you have to enter values for the **Application enrollment token, .pfx file,** and **Application package containing signed company portal .xap** fields, as shown in the following screenshot:

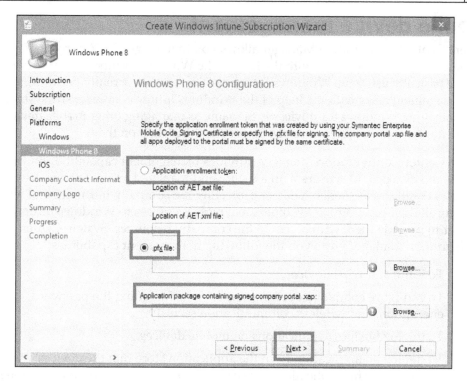

° For iOS devices, you have to enter a value for the **APNs certificate** field, as shown here:

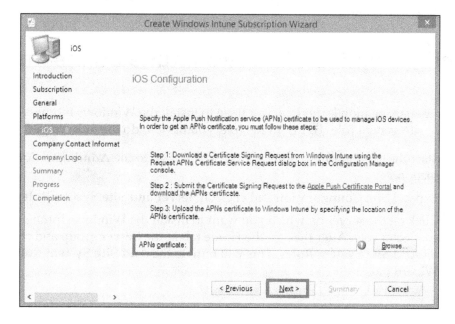

Mobile device management

System Center Configuration Manager allows you to manage iOS, Android, Windows Phone, and Windows devices with the help of the Windows Intune service. Although you are basically using the Windows Intune service, you are actually performing all the management tasks with the help of the Windows Intune connector site system role. Managing Windows 8.1 devices is the same as managing other mobile devices that do not have the Configuration Manager client installed on them.

System Center Configuration Manager provides management capabilities for mobile devices and also provides users with a secure and managed access to company resources. With this approach, you are protecting the company resources and letting users enroll their company or even personal mobile devices to Windows Intune in order to provide them with access to the company resources. System Center Configuration Manager gives you the following management capabilities:

- To retire and wipe devices.
- To configure compliance settings on devices, including the password, encryption, and wireless communication security.
- To deploy business applications on mobile devices.
- To deploy an application from the application store that the devices' platform connects to. The application store can be Windows Store, Windows Phone Store, Google Play, or App Store.
- To collect the software and hardware inventories.
- To create reports.

Configuring the Windows Intune connector role

In order to manage mobile devices, you have to install the Windows Intune connector site system role. To install the role, you have to do the following:

1. Start the Configuration Manager console and go to the **Administration** section.

2. Expand **Site Configuration** and click on **Server and Site System Roles**.

3. Click on the server on which you want to install the Windows Intune connector role. After that, go the **Home** tab in the **Server** group and click on **Add Site System Roles**. This will initiate the **Add Site System Roles Wizard** page.

4. On the **System Role Selection** page, select **Windows Intune Connector** and click on **Next**.

Mobile device enrollment

Mobile device enrollment establishes a relationship of trust between a user, a device, and the Windows Intune service. Users can also enroll their privately owned mobile devices. Every mobile device platform requires a unique and different configuration so that devices running this platform can be enrolled to Windows Intune. To find out how to enroll different mobile device platforms, follow this link:

`http://technet.microsoft.com/en-us/library/jj884158.aspx#bkmk_enroll`

Mobile application delivery

The Windows Intune subscription can be used to deliver applications to your mobile devices and their respective platforms. What follows is a list describing which type of device the link will be used for:

* Mobile application delivery for iOS:

  `http://blogs.technet.com/b/privatecloud/archive/2013/11/21/`
  `mobile-application-delivery-with-system-center-configuration-`
  `manager-2012-r2-and-windows-intune-part-2-of-5.aspx`

* Mobile application delivery for an Android operating system:

  `http://blogs.technet.com/b/privatecloud/archive/2014/04/18/`
  `mobile-application-delivery-with-system-center-configuration-`
  `manager-2012-r2-and-windows-intune-part-5.aspx`

* Mobile application delivery for a Windows Phone 8 operating system:

  `http://blogs.technet.com/b/privatecloud/archive/2014/03/24/`
  `mobile-application-delivery-with-system-center-configuration-`
  `manager-2012-r2-and-windows-intune-part-4.aspx`

* Mobile application delivery for Windows 8 and RT operating systems:

  `http://blogs.technet.com/b/privatecloud/archive/2013/12/17/`
  `mobile-application-delivery-with-system-center-configuration-`
  `manager-2012-r2-and-windows-intune-part-3-of-5.aspx`

  `http://blogs.technet.com/b/privatecloud/archive/2014/02/28/`
  `mobile-application-delivery-with-system-center-configuration-`
  `manager-2012-r2-and-windows-intune-part-3b.aspx`

Cloud distribution points

A cloud distribution point is a fallback distribution point for the Configuration Manager clients and supports most of the content types. To create a cloud distribution point, you need a Windows Azure subscription, a DNS server, and certificates. For your production environment, you can use the Azure pricing calculator to calculate your subscription fee at `http://azure.microsoft.com/en-us/pricing/calculator/?scenario=full`.

Starting with System Center Configuration Manager SP1, you can use a Windows Azure cloud service to host a distribution point server. When you deploy a cloud-based distribution point server, you configure the client settings and through them, enable users and devices to access the content. You also have to specify a primary site that will manage the content transfer to the cloud-based distribution point. Additionally, you need to specify the thresholds for the amount of content that you want to store on the distribution point and the amount of content that you want to enable clients to transfer from the distribution point. Based on these thresholds, the Configuration Manager can raise alerts that warn you when the combined amount of content that you have stored on the distribution point is near the specified storage amount, or when the transfer of data by the clients is close to the threshold that you defined.

The following features are supported by both on-premise and cloud-based distribution points:

- The management of cloud-based distribution points individually or as members of distribution point groups
- A cloud-based distribution point can be used as a fallback content location
- You receive support for both intranet- and Internet-based clients

A cloud-based distribution point provides the following additional benefits:

- The content that is sent to the cloud-based distribution point is encrypted by Configuration Manager before the Configuration Manager sends it to Windows Azure
- In Windows Azure, you can manually scale the cloud service to meet the changing demands for content request by clients, without the requirement to install and provision additional distribution points
- The cloud-based distribution point supports the download of content by clients that are configured for Windows BranchCache

A cloud-based distribution point has the following limitations:

- You cannot use a cloud-based distribution point to host software update packages.

- You cannot use a cloud-based distribution point for PXE-enabled or multicast-enabled deployments.

- Clients are not offered a cloud-based distribution point as a content location for a task sequence that is deployed using the **Download content locally when needed by running task sequence** deployment option. However, task sequences that are deployed using the **Download all content locally before starting task sequence** deployment option can use a cloud-based distribution point as a valid content location.

- A cloud-based distribution point does not support packages that run from the distribution point. All content must be downloaded by the client and then run locally.

- A cloud-based distribution point does not support the streaming of applications by using Application Virtualization or similar programs.

- Prestaged content is not supported. The primary site Distribution Manager that is used for distribution point management does all the content transfers to the distribution point.

- A cloud-based distribution point cannot be configured as a pull-distribution point.

To configure a cloud-based distribution point, follow these steps:

1. Create a management certificate and install it on the site server. This certificate establishes a trust relationship between the site server and Windows Azure.

2. Create a cloud distribution point service certificate and install it on the site server.

3. Create a Windows Azure subscription and import the previously created management certificate in Windows Azure through the management portal.

4. Install a cloud distribution point role in Configuration Manager.

5. Set up the client settings to allow Configuration Manager clients to use the cloud-based distribution point.

6. Create a record in your DNS with the IP address of the cloud distribution point.

Cloud distribution points – prerequisites

A cloud-based distribution point has the following prerequisites:

- A Windows Azure subscription.

- A self-signed or PKI management certificate for communication between the Configuration Manager primary site server and the Windows Azure Cloud Service.

- A service certificate (PKI) that Configuration Manager clients will use in order to connect to the cloud-based distribution points and also to download content from these distribution points using secure transfer or HTTPS.

- Before users and devices can access the content on a cloud-based distribution point, a device or a user has to receive the client setting for cloud services of **Allow access to cloud distribution points** set to **Yes**. By default, this value is set to **No**.

- A client must be able to resolve the name of the cloud service, which requires a **Domain Name System** (**DNS**) alias and CNAME record, in your DNS namespace.

- A client must have Internet access in order to use the cloud-based distribution point.

Creating certificates

Use the following link to create the needed certificates for the Cloud distribution point creation:

```
http://technet.microsoft.com/en-us/library/230dfec0-bddb-4429-a5db-30020e881f1e#BKMK_clouddp2008_cm2012
```

Importing the certificates in Windows Azure

First, what you need to do is log in to your Windows Azure subscription. To do this, you have to perform the following steps:

1. Go to `https://manage.windowsazure.com`.

2. After you log in, go to **SETTINGS** from the menu on the left-hand side, as shown in the following screenshot:

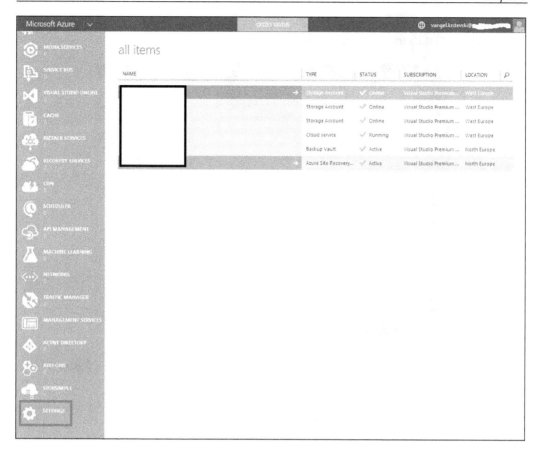

3. Click on **MANAGEMENT CERTIFICATES**, as shown here:

4. Upload the management certificate that you created for the site server, as shown in the following screenshot:

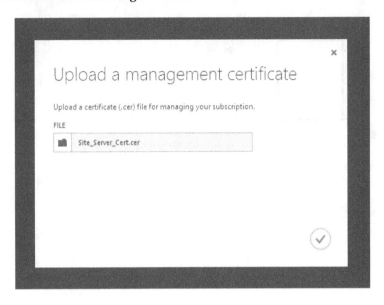

5. After the import, you will be able to see the certificate in the list of imported **MANAGEMENT CERTIFICATES**, as shown here:

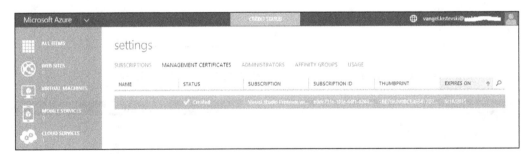

Creating the cloud distribution point

In order to create the cloud distribution point, you have to do the following:

1. Start the System Center Configuration Manager console.

2. Navigate to **Administration** | **Hierarchy Configuration** | **Cloud Services** | **Cloud Distribution Points**, as shown in the following screenshot:

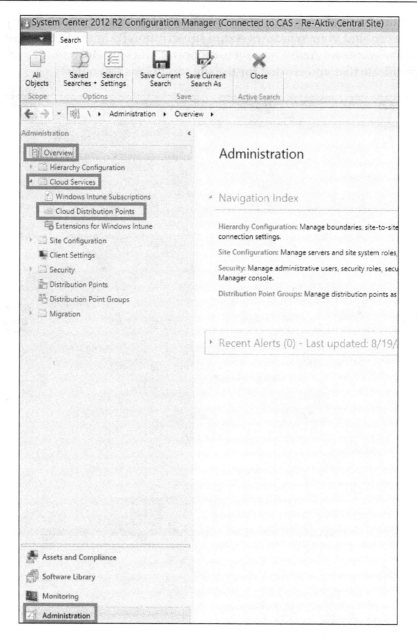

3. From the ribbon bar, click on **Create Cloud Distribution Point**.

4. On the **General** page, you have to enter the Windows Azure subscription ID. You can find your Windows Azure subscription ID in the **Settings** section of the Windows Azure management portal. Click on **Browse...** to select the certificate that you created for the site server, as shown here:

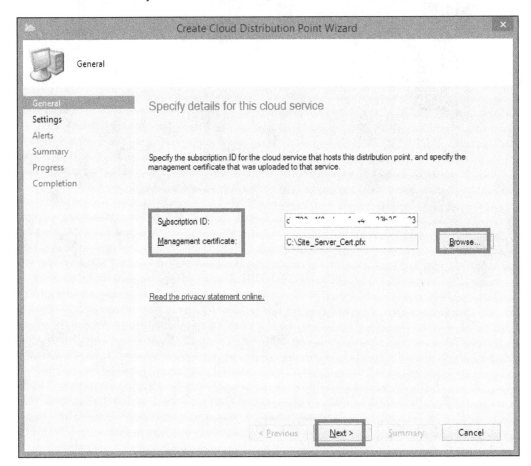

5. On the **Settings** page, select the region, for example, **West Europe**. Click on **Browse…** and import the cloud distribution point service certificate, as shown in the next screenshot:

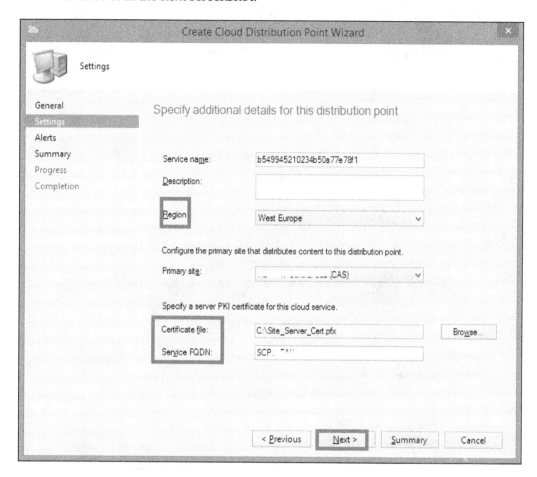

6. On the **Alerts** page, you can configure the settings about the threshold levels of your cloud distribution point. These levels are important because they can alert you when levels drop below a certain level that you have defined. For the purpose of this project, just click on **Next**:

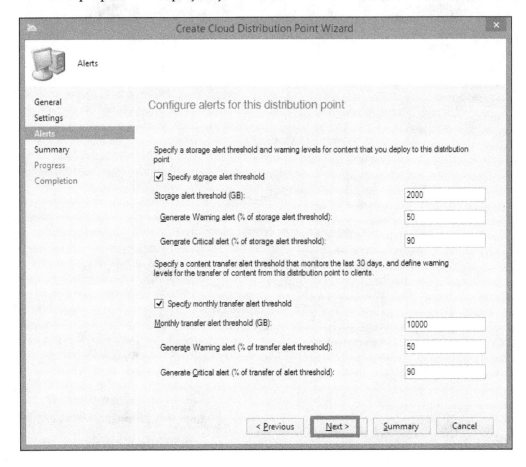

7. Review all the settings in the **Summary** page and click on **Next** to start the cloud distribution point's installation process.

8. After the Cloud distribution point is created, you will be able to see it in the list of **Cloud Distribution Points** in the System Center Configuration Manager console, as shown here:

Cloud Distribution Points 1 items							
Icon	Service Name	Cloud Service Name	Region	Status	Storage Quota (GB)	Transfer Quota (GB)	Description
	SCP.REAKTIV.IN	b549945210234b50a77e78f1	West Europe	Provisioning	2,000	10,000	

Configuring DNS for the cloud distribution point

For clients to download content from a cloud distribution point, a DNS record must exist for the cloud distribution point's IP address. You can do this by adding a CNAME record in your DNS server that points to the site URL of the Windows Azure Cloud Service. The FQDN of your Windows Azure Cloud Service can be found by proceeding with the following steps:

1. Log in to your Windows Azure subscription.

2. Select **Cloud Services** from the menu on the left-hand side.

3. From the list of cloud services, click on the service name that represents your cloud distribution point. This will open the cloud service dashboard. The site URL information can be found on the right-hand side of the dashboard, as shown in the following screenshot:

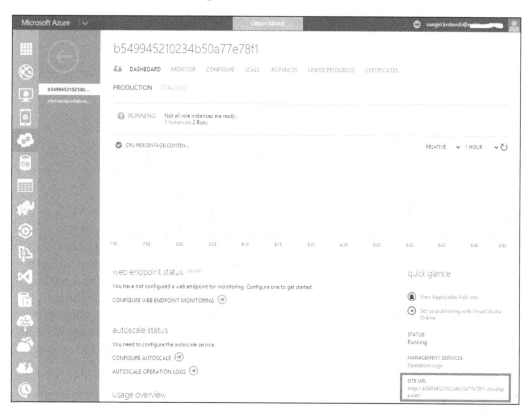

4. Open your DNS server and create the CNAME record. For the alias name, enter `CloudDP` and for the FQDN of the target host, enter the site URL of your Windows Azure, shown as follows:

Summary

In this chapter, we saw the benefits of the Microsoft Public Cloud, specifically Windows Azure. We saw how we can integrate System Center Configuration Manager 2012 R2 with Windows Azure and how to configure a cloud distribution point. The main benefit of a cloud distribution point is that it can work as a backup distribution point. We also saw how we can use System Center Configuration Manager 2012 R2 to deliver applications to different mobile device platforms. We also learned how to connect the Configuration Manager to Windows Intune in order to provide mobile device management and application deployment and to ensure secure and managed access to company resources.

The next chapter will take a look at the different ways you can secure the access to your Configuration Manager infrastructure by defining security roles. The chapter also discusses different ways in which you can back up the Configuration Manager's configuration.

7

Security and Backup

A very important part of maintaining a healthy and functional system is to ensure its integrity through backup and recovery processes. All production systems should have established backup and recovery procedures in place and should have System Center Configuration Manager 2012 as well. You must maintain data integrity and currency, and Configuration Manager provides a number of maintenance tasks that assist you with this.

Information is the most important asset belonging to most organizations today. To ensure information integrity, confidentiality and resource availability are the most important values for effective systems management. This chapter will discuss the role of Configuration Manager in securing your environment. It presents the new role-based administration model and takes into consideration the proper delegation of administrative roles in order to reduce the risk of an accidental misuse of rights. Critical consideration should be given to protect the Configuration Manager infrastructure from being compromised and used against you. In this chapter, we will take a look at security for Configuration Manager servers, clients, and network communication.

Administrative users

To give users or security groups management access to Configuration Manager, you need to create an administrative user in Configuration Manager and also specify the Windows account of the user or user's group. After this, you must assign at least one security role and one security scope for that administrative user. To create a new administrative user, follow these steps:

1. Open the **Configuration Manager** console and go to the **Administration** section.

2. Expand **Security** and click on **Administrative Users**.

3. Under the **Home** tab on the ribbon bar, in the **Create** group, click on **Add User or Group**.

4. Click on **Browse** and then select the user account or the group to be used for the administrative user.

5. Next, you need to associate a security role with the administrative user. Click on **Add** to open a list of the available security roles. You can choose between the following options:

   ° **All securable objects that are relevant to their associated security roles**: This option associates the administrative user with the **All** security scope and the root level, which are built-in collections for **All Systems** and **All Users and User Groups**. The security roles assigned to the user define access to objects. The new objects that this administrative user creates are assigned to the default security scope.

   ° **Only securable objects in specified security scopes or collections**: By default, this option associates the administrative user with the default security scope and the **All Systems** and **All Users and User Groups** collections. However, the actual security scopes and collections are limited to those that are associated with the account that you used to create the new administrative user. This option supports the addition or removal of security scopes and collections to customize the administrative scope of the administrative user.

6. If you choose the first option, then just click on **OK**. If you choose the second option, you can click on **Add to select additional security scopes**. When you finish adding the scopes, click on **OK**.

Security roles

A security role is a set of permissions that allow a user to perform tasks. System Center Configuration Manager 2012 has built-in security roles that cover common responsibilities. You have the opportunity to create custom roles according to particular needs for your organization. Security roles are visible through the entire System Center Configuration Manager hierarchy and are replicated for all the sites.

Built-in roles

The built-in security roles consist of a set of permissions required for typical IT administrator tasks. If some of these roles meet your requirements and needs, you can assign your Configuration Manager administrators to them. These built-in security roles can only be viewed but cannot be modified. To access the built-in roles, go to the **Administration** section of the console, click on **Security**, and then select **Security Roles**. To avoid the risk of someone with administrative access to Configuration Manager misusing their permissions, you should follow these recommendations:

- Perform a separation of duties, where it can be done, in order to make it more difficult to misuse administrative permissions. When someone performs an improper activity, the level of effort and risk of getting caught is much lower than it will be if collusion with others were necessary. The extent to which you choose to separate the responsibilities for some tasks depends on the security requirements and available resources. For example, you can assign the Application Administrator role and the Application Deployment Manager role to two different individuals.

- Configure the least privileges that are necessary for each administrator to execute their responsibilities. If you assign a broad range of privileges to users or administrators, you increase the chances of compromising the system and data. A good practice is to review the permissions in the built-in roles and create custom roles with only the permissions needed. Also, keep in mind that you can never exclude human errors, such as deploying a task sequence to all the systems by mistake.

The Full Administrator role provides unrestricted access to all Configuration Manager operations. If your administration model separates security administration from the operational tasks, then you can assign the Security Administrator and the Operations Administrator roles to separate users. Keep in mind that you must have one user with the Full Administrator role.

Custom roles

You can create a custom role by copying the existing role and editing the permissions for the copy. This is how you can create a custom security role:

1. Go to the **Administration** section of the console, then go to **Security**, and then select the **Security Roles** node.

2. Right-click on the role that you want to customize and select **Copy**.

3. In the **Copy Security Role** dialog, enter a name for the new role.

 You can export a custom role and then import it in a different hierarchy.

Security scopes

Security roles define the operations that a user can perform on each class of objects. You can further limit the administrative user by assigning the securable objects that users have for each role:

- To specify the set of devices and users that the administrative user can manage, assign specific device collections or user collections to the administrator. You can assign one or more collections to each user. You can also assign a different set of collections to a user for each role that the user holds. By default, the **All Systems** and **All Users** collections are assigned to each administrative user.

- To specify the other sets of objects that an administrator can manage, assign specific security scopes to the administrator. A security scope is essentially a container that contains one or more types of securable objects. You can assign one or more security scopes to each administrative user. You can also assign a different set of security scopes to a user for each role that the user holds. The default security scope is assigned to each administrator by default.

- Permissions on some types of objects apply to all types of instances and cannot be restricted by the collection's membership or security scope.

When you create a new administrative user, first you need add security roles to the user. This gives permissions to perform different actions. After that, you need to assign a specific security scope. A security scope defines to which objects the newly created user can apply the actions that they are permitted with the security role.

There are two built-in security scopes: **All** and **Default**. Administrators who have the **All** security scope can administer all the objects related to their role. Built-in instances and newly created instances of securable objects are also assigned to the **Default** security scope. Here's the procedure to create additional security scopes:

1. Go to the **Administration** section of the console, select **Security**, and then right-click on **Security Scopes**.

2. Select **Create Security Scope**.

3. In the **Create Security Scope** dialog, enter the security scope name and description and then click on **OK**.

After creating a new securable object, you can set its security scopes. Follow these steps to do this:

1. Locate the object in the Configuration Manager console and right-click on it. You can use the standard *Ctrl + Shift* option to select multiple objects for which you want to specify the same scope.

2. Select **Set Security Scopes**.

3. In the **Create Security Scope** dialog, select one or more scopes that you would like to associate with the objects and click on **OK**.

Security scopes generally eliminate the requirement to use sites as a security boundary. You can choose to remove the **All Systems** and **All Users** collections from all the administrative users. This means that users can only see and manage resources in collections to which you give them access. Giving access to the **All Systems** and **All Users** collections simplifies the administration by eliminating the requirement to grant access to individual collections. Keep in mind that when you create a collection, you have to base the new collection on an existing collection. Users with access to the original collection inherit access to the collections that are based on it.

Associating security scopes and collections with individual roles

An administrative user who has assigned more than one role might have the same security scopes and collections available for all the roles, or they might have different security scopes and collections available for each role. For example, an endpoint security group manages software updates and Endpoint Protection for both servers and desktops, but compliance settings manage updates only on end-user systems. To prevent this group from deploying compliance settings to servers, remove the **All Systems** collection and assign a collection consisting of desktops and laptops only. To prevent this group from deploying the compliance settings for a server to users' systems, remove the **Default** security scope and add a security scope consisting of settings that are designed for specific systems. Perform the following steps:

1. Go to the **Administration** section of the console, select **Security**, and click on **Administrative Users**.

2. Double-click on the user you want to customize.

3. In the **Security Scopes** tab, select the radio button for **Associate assigned security roles with specific security scopes and collections**. Select the role you want to edit and click on **Edit** to open the **Edit Security Scope** dialog.

4. In the **Edit Security Scope** dialog, select the **All Systems** collection and the **Default Security** scope and click on **Remove**. Click on the **Add** button and choose **Collection**. Select **Device Collections** from the upper-left drop-down list and check the box for the appropriate collection. Then, click on **OK**.

5. Click on **Add** and select **Security Scope**. Select the appropriate scope and click on **OK**.

Preventing unauthorized administrative access

In addition to assigning users to appropriate roles, it is important to prevent the unauthorized or inappropriate use of administrative access. What follows is an explanation of how an attacker can gain rights on Configuration Manager:

- An attacker can alter Configuration Manager security through Active Directory. Configuration Manager roles are assigned to Active Directory users and groups. Anyone who gains the requisite Active Directory privileges can add themselves to a group or can reset the password of a user account to get access to Configuration Manager.

- An attacker can alter Configuration Manager security by directly modifying a **Role Based Administration** (**RBA**) object in the site database.

- An attacker can steal the credentials or hijack the session of a legitimate administrator.

Protection against these risks requires effective security at the Active Directory and database layers and the maintenance of a strong auditing policy.

The Active Directory security

The following are some ways in which you can protect groups and user accounts with privileged access to Configuration Manager:

- **Restrict the rights to manage administrative accounts and groups to a small group of senior administrators**: You should remove any delegated rights to groups, such as helpdesk personnel. You should consider moving administrative accounts and groups to specific organizational units in order to simplify security management.

- **Set auditing to record any changes to these user accounts and groups**: Audit policies are defined in the **Default Domain Controller** group policy by navigating to **Computer Configuration | Windows Settings | Security Settings | Local Policy | Audit Policy**. Events specified through the audit policy are recorded in the local security event log of the Domain Controller on which the event occurs. Some specific audit settings you might want to consider include:

    ° **Audit account management**: Events in the account management category include sensitive operations such as getting the password of a user account or adding a member to a group.

    ° **Audit directory service access**: Events in the directory service access category include modifications to specific AD objects such as users or groups. When you enable the directory service access auditing category through the group policy, you also need to turn on the auditing of the specific objects. You can find more information on directory service auditing at `http://technet.microsoft.com/enus/library/cc731607.aspx`.

- **Provide ongoing education on security best practices to administrators**: Some security breaches have targeted administrators with phishing or other social engineering methods. A hacker who tricks an administrator into clicking on the wrong link or attaching the wrong device to the system has a good chance of compromising the network. IT administrators should always use a no-privileged account to log on to the local workstation and to perform activities such as checking e-mails or browsing on the Internet.

- **Extra attention should be paid to securing administrative workstations and other systems where the console is installed**: It is important to disable the password caching on administrative workstations and to locate these systems in areas that are physically secure and not easily accessible.

To view more Active Directory security best practices, visit `http://technet.microsoft.com/en-us/library/cc773365.aspx`.

Securing access at the database level

System Center Configuration Manager 2012 supports SQL Server in either the mixed mode or the Windows authentication mode. You should use Windows authentication for all site database servers. Windows authentication provides much stronger account controls and authentication mechanisms. Database logins should be granted to Active Directory users and groups rather than local users and groups on the database server.

As with any administrative access, you should assign SQL Server access on a least privilege basis. It is important to limit access to privileged server roles, such as `sysadmin` and `securityadmin`. Generally speaking, there is no reason to assign database roles for the site database directly to users, and you should avoid doing this. You can use a SQL Server hosted on the site server, but if possible, use a dedicated SQL Server that is not shared with other applications. This will reduce the number of users needing access to the server as well as the overall attack surface of the database server. You can find more information on SQL security at the following link:

`http://msdn.microsoft.com/en-us/library/ms144228.aspx`

Another tool that you can use is the SQL Server best practices analyzer, which can be found at `http://www.microsoft.com/en-us/download/details.aspx?id=15289`.

Auditing the Configuration Manager's administrative actions

Administrative actions ensure that the audit trails for all security-sensitive actions are properly preserved and that regular audits of your IT environment review Configuration Manager's activity. Any environment will consist of a group of individuals with the authority to carry out the actions required to administer information systems. Although you cannot generally block the administrative group from all the opportunities to misuse their authority, increasing the chance of detection reduces the chance of repeated and ongoing security breaches. Auditing is an area in which the separation of duties should be strictly enforced; you should not rely on the administrators who are responsible for normal operations as the sole source of data or on the reports used for auditing purposes.

Configuration Manager generates status messages of the type **Audit** to provide an audit record of certain security-sensitive operations. The SMS provider also generates audit messages when a user creates, modifies, or deletes a Configuration Manager object or changes the associated security scope for an object. Audit messages for object modifications indicate the user making the change, the target object class and object ID, and the details indicating when and how the change occurred. Specific attribute changes are not included. An important auditing consideration is the retention period for auditing records. You might be required to retain the audit data for a specified time to meet regulatory requirements.

Most enterprises use a **Security Information and Event Management (SIEM)** solution to aggregate and correlate data from various security information and event sources. SIEM solutions monitor an activity in real time and allow rapid detection and response to suspicious activity. If you have such a system, it is necessary to connect all the audit data to the SIEM solution. The site database stores status messages in the StatusMessages table. When you want to extract information from the Configuration Manager database, always use views instead of tables. It is important to log and audit sensitive actions at every layer of the infrastructure. Auditing the following systems will help you to protect the Configuration Manager environment:

- Active Directory
- Site systems
- SQL Server
- Network devices

Securing the Configuration Manager infrastructure

Effective management and monitoring can greatly improve the security of your Configuration Manager environment. A potential compromise of the management application is a threat that you cannot allow and ignore. Their target includes every type of business, and their objective is to steal valuable intellectual property and business secrets for military and economic advantage. These attackers often attempt to compromise Domain Controllers. As companies increase their attention toward securing Domain Controllers, management systems become the next point of attack.

The critical infrastructure components that could be the subject of attacks include Configuration Manager site systems, accounts used by Configuration Manager, intersite and intrasite communication, Windows Intune, and other infrastructure services that Configuration Manager relies on. Before securing these components, spend some time in designing and planning the Configuration Manager infrastructure.

In order to keep your Configuration Manager infrastructure up to date and to protect it against unwanted attacks, you can deploy Configuration Manager Servicing Extension. This is a tool released by Microsoft, and it helps IT administrators by providing useful information for maintaining the Configuration Manager infrastructure. To find out more about this tool, follow this link:

```
http://msincic.wordpress.com/2014/07/16/configuration-manager-
servicing-extension-for-sccm-2012-sp1-and-r2/
```

Building security into your hierarchy

Always consider your organization's security requirements throughout the life cycle of the Configuration Manager implementation. Keep in mind the following points:

- **Active Directory consideration**: Configuration Manager sites and hierarchies can span more than one Active Directory forest. This might compromise your Active Directory's security. The forest is a security boundary in Active Directory. Allowing administrators and systems in one forest to configure site systems and administering clients in a second forest can violate the autonomy of the forest in which the managed systems reside. A best practice is to isolate each Configuration Manager hierarchy in a single forest. This is possible only in theory and with regards security considerations because setting up and maintaining separate Configuration Manager hierarchies for every Active Directory forest is not ideal.

- **Configuration Manager site selection**: The fewer sites you have, the easier it is to maintain security. Additional sites increase the number of site servers, site databases, and intersite communication links that you need to administer and secure. Sometimes, you might consider using dedicated sites for specific security needs. This decision will add an additional overhead to IT administrators because they will have to administer more than one site.

- **Site system role assignment**: It is important to move client-facing roles such as the management point and the distribution point off the site server. You can reduce the risk of a network attack by restricting client access to only those server roles that require it. The site server and site database server are the most important roles in your site, and allowing clients to establish network connections to these systems is a risk. Separating server roles generally reduces the requirement for services and open network ports on each system. You need to weigh this advantage against the effort to support and secure additional site systems. If you install **Internet Information Services (IIS)** on a server, it will increase the attack surface. Because of this, you should generally separate server roles requiring IIS from those that do not. You also need to separate the fallback status point server role from all other system roles. The most important security consideration for assigning system roles is to avoid using systems that host other applications as site systems, especially those with applications based on IIS or SQL Server. If your web and database applications are poorly written, they can be the targets of attackers. Installing a distribution point role on a server that is used for file and print services is a much lower risk.

- **Server placement**: All site systems should be deployed to locations that are as secure as possible in terms of physical and network access. An attacker with physical access to a site system or administrative workstation can compromise your system. Network traffic should be restricted to that necessary for Configuration Manager operations and basic server functions. If possible, you can place the site server and site database server in a secure management zone that is not easily accessible from systems with lower security requirements. If an administrator needs to reach these systems from a less secure zone, they can use a Virtual Private Network to connect to the systems in the higher security zone.

Securing site systems

Consider your Configuration Manager site server and site systems as the most security-sensitive assets in your organization at par with the Domain Controllers. All the basic controls applicable to such systems should be applied to your site systems. You can implement some of the following controls to protect the site systems.

Physical security and hardware selection

You must choose the most secure location and hardware available for your site systems. Site servers and site database servers should be located in secure data centers. You need to balance security concerns with your other requirements as you consider the placement of client-facing systems, such as distribution points. Server hardware often provides functionality such as alarms that alert you when they detect an open chassis or modification to the hardware. Choose hardware with the maximum reliability and redundancy for systems with high availability requirements.

System software security

Choose the most recent version of Microsoft Windows that is consistent with your system requirements and install all the service packs and security patches. Security awareness and technology is reflected in the design of modern operating systems, and each version of Windows has gained numerous security enhancements over its predecessor. Often, this accumulation of small enhancements can make as much difference, or more, as the more highly publicized features. In addition to OS patches, you should keep system components, such as BIOS and firmware, current and regularly update all the drivers and applications.

Attack surface reduction and server hardening

A basic principle for securing any system is to reduce the number of potential vulnerabilities by eliminating unnecessary services, accounts, applications, network shares, open network ports, and so on. In addition to reducing the attack surface of your servers, harden them by modifying the default settings, such as requiring the use of more secure network protocols and eliminating access to certain GUI. The key to reducing the attack surface without reducing functionalities is to determine these features as unnecessary to the system so that you can turn them off. Microsoft has a set of tools that greatly simplify attack surface reduction. These tools are:

- **Windows Security Configuration Wizard**: The System Center 2012 Configuration Manager template for the Windows Security Configuration Wizard is included as part of the Configuration Manager toolkit. You can download the toolkit from `http://www.microsoft.com/en-us/download/details.aspx?id=29265`.

- **SQL Server surface and configuration for SQL Server 2008**: Use this tool to turn off unnecessary Microsoft SQL Server features. To find out more about this tool, visit `http://www.mssqltips.com/sqlservertip/1673/where-is-the-surface-area-configuration-tool-in-sql-server-2008/`.

- **Policy-based management for SQL Server 2008 R2**: Use this tool to turn off unnecessary Microsoft SQL Server features. To find out more about this tool, visit `http://technet.microsoft.com/en-us/library/bb522466(v=sql.105).aspx`.

- **Configuration Manager compliance settings**.

Security software

You should run antivirus software on all the systems in your environment and update virus signatures on a regular basis. However, be careful when running antivirus software on Configuration Manager site systems. You should make a list of the excluded folders and file types that should be established in order to prevent interruptions to Configuration Manager. Traditional antivirus software compares files and processes them against a database of signatures that are known as malware. Signature-based malware detection is reasonably effective against widely deployed viruses, spyware, and other malware, and is an essential part of an antimalware strategy. Some antivirus programs also use behavior-based detection that responds to suspicious activities, such as a program opening a network port. Additional enhancements include real-time feeds of threat intelligence information from the Internet.

Even with these enhancements, traditional malware protection is only partially effective in detecting targeted threats, including APTs. Many organizations with high security requirements are incorporating application whitelisting programs into their malware protection strategy. Application whitelisting allows only specific processes to run on the system. Deploying application whitelisting technology requires you to have methods to update all of the system components.

Software firewalls, such as the Windows firewall, provide protection from network-based attacks. Go through all the rules and make sure that they are properly configured. In environments that require high security, you might choose to use specialized host intrusion prevention software in order to provide an additional layer of protection by detecting and blocking a more extensive range of suspicious process activity such as nonstandard memory access methods. File integrity monitoring software protects critical files from alteration. Security programs are intrusive by nature. They often consume significant amounts of system resources and sometimes block legitimate activity. You should test and adjust the security software settings in your test environment and monitor the impact of security software in your production environment. To improve the system's performance and availability, it is sometimes advisable to exclude certain directories from virus scanning. Exclusions are typically applied to files that are frequently accessed or generally locked during normal operations that are not common in order to introduce a malware in the environment. Any scanning exclusions that you create can introduce a potential weakness.

You should have a process to respond to events from the security software, such as malware detection and blocked activity. If you find false-positive detections, evaluate their impact on the system's functionality and modify the security software settings as required. If you suspect that virus scanning is affecting your system or application's stability and performance, you can use the Process Monitor to determine which files your virus scanner is opening.

If you see files that are frequently scanned, you might consider excluding them. Some antivirus applications allow you to apply different on-access scanning exclusions based on the process that is accessing the files.

Securing the site system's local administration

The built-in local administrators group on any Windows system has complete and unrestricted access to the computer. Even without specific administrative rights within Configuration Manager, a member of the administrators group on a Configuration Manager site system can potentially alter the files, registry settings, or other items related to the system's configuration in ways that will affect Configuration Manager. By default, the Domain Admins group for the local domain is part of the local administrators group. Consider removing the Domain Admins group and replacing it with the appropriate Active Directory group that is directly responsibility for the server administration of the site system. For nonclient facing systems, you might also want to consider removing the Domain Users group from the local Users group. The remaining built-in groups such as Backup Operators and Power Users should not contain any members unless required for your administrative processes. You should generally not create local users or groups on site systems other than those required by Configuration Manager. As with all Windows systems, rename the built-in administrator account, set a strong password for this account, and use appropriate procedures to manage access to the account password. You should also disable the built-in guest account. You can configure most of these settings locally or through the group policy.

 The local administrator account is used to log on to a machine that was removed from the domain. In this case, the account name reverts to the state before the domain group policy was applied.

Just as auditing the Active Directory administration helps detect the misuse of domain-level administrative privileges, auditing actions by administrators on site systems is an important part of your control framework. Use a group policy to enable the appropriate auditing. These are some of the auditing categories that you should consider enabling on site systems:

- **Audit account management**: The local user account and group policy will rarely change, so auditing the local account management on site systems will generate a low overhead.

- **Audit policy change**: As with account management, policy changes should rarely occur locally on the server. However, when changes occur, you need to know about it.

- **Audit object access**: You should audit changes to the files or registry that might affect Configuration Manager.

Securing the site database

The site database server is the heart of your Configuration Manager site. Its security is at least as important as the one on the site server. You should use a dedicated SQL Server for each primary site or locate the database on the site server.

Configure SQL Server to use Windows authentication only and enable logging for at least the failed logon attempts. Use a low-privilege domain account for the SQL Server start-up account rather than running SQL Server under a local system. If you run in a low-privilege account, you need to register the service principal name for the server in the Active Directory. This service principal name is used to locate SQL services.

Configuration Manager's network security

Network-based attacks are commonly used to steal data or carry out malicious tasks. These are some network attacks that can be launched at Configuration Manager sites, site systems, and clients, as follows:

- **Misdirection attacks**: This is when a client or site system is provided with the wrong name or IP address for the partner with which it needs to communicate. You should secure the name resolution services to avoid this attack.

- **Spoofing attacks**: This is when a rogue system impersonates the actual system. To defeat spoofing attacks, all communications have to be authenticated.

- **Eavesdropping**: This occurs when an attacker intercepts network traffic, thus gaining access to confidential information. To avoid this, use data encryption.

- **Man in the middle**: These occur when an attacker steals, alters, or interrupts communications by routing data through an intermediate node. You can defeat these attacks by mutual authentication.

- **Denial of Service**: These occur when an attacker uses large amounts of data to crash systems. A resilient network infrastructure and fault-tolerant service delivery is the best defense against such attacks.

Client-to-server communications security

Clients communicate with most site systems using either HTTP or HTTPS. An HTTPS communication requires a PKI certificate. A client configured to support HTTPS will select a site system using HTTPS, if there is one available. Here are the advantages of using HTTPS:

- HTTPS traffic is encrypted
- HTTPS implements mutual authentication
- Lowers the risk of impersonation attacks

Server-to-server communications security

All communication between site systems within a site is authenticated using either a PKI certificate or a self-signed certificate. An intrasite server communication is not encrypted. Always consider the sensitivity of the data exchanged between site systems and the risk of server-to-server communication being compromised. This risk is higher for systems in less-protected network zones such as DMZ. If you think that server-to-server communication should also be encrypted, consider implementing IPSec between servers.

The site server should have the highest level of system, network, and physical security that you can provide. There might be instances where you might not be able to provide the same level of security for all the site systems. If that's the case, then consider enabling the **Require the site server to initiate connections to this site system** option. This is mainly introduced because of potential firewall restrictions in a DMZ zone. In this scenario, the server located in the DMZ is untrusted. This will only allow traffic that is initiated by trusted systems, that is, the site server.

Site-to-site communications security

Sites share data using database replication and file-based replication. Database replication uses a self-signed certificate to authenticate the replication connections and to sign and encrypt data. The certificate's trust mechanism ensures that only Configuration Manager database servers can participate in the database replication for that hierarchy. File-based replication implements data signing, but it does not offer data encryption. If you want to encrypt file-based replication, you should implement IPSec between site servers. You can read more about how to configure IPSec between servers at `http://technet.microsoft.com/en-us/library/cc730656.aspx`.

Site and SQL Server backups

System Center Configuration Manager 2012 includes out-of-the-box tasks to assist you in maintaining your environment. One of these tasks is the backup site server maintenance task, which simplifies the backup process of the Configuration Manager environment.

Backing up Configuration Manager

You can find the site maintenance tasks in the **Administration** section of the Configuration Manager console. Navigate to **Overview** | **Site Configuration** | **Sites** | **Site Code** | **Site Name** | **Site Maintenance**, as shown in the following screenshot:

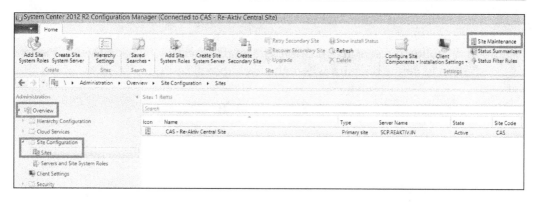

To enable the Backup Site Server task and to configure it to back up your site, you have to do the following:

1. Select the **Backup Site Server** task located in the **Maintenance tasks** section of the Configuration Manager console. From the list, select **Backup Site Server** and click on **Edit...** to open the **Properties** page, as shown here:

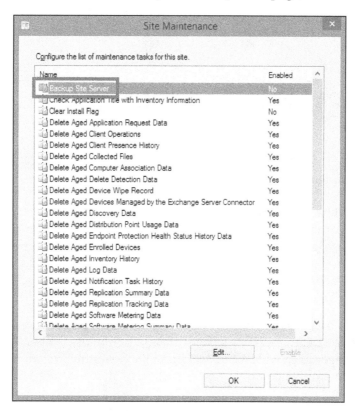

2. The first option of the Backup Site Server's **Properties** page is to enable the task by selecting the checkbox at the top of the **Properties** page, as shown in the following screenshot. After you enable the task, click on the **Set Paths** button to define the path where the backup will reside.

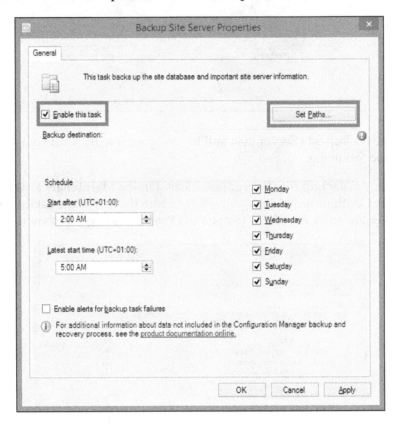

A recommended backup strategy is to use a daily backup and to send the backup data to a UNC path that is not on any Configuration Manager server system. Data backups are done daily, and the backups should be retained for at least one month. This will minimize the risk that the site server will fail. These backups will be overwritten each time the backup runs. It is important to implement your own custom strategy in order to archive the previous backups.

You should also back up the files required to restore the operating system on the site server in the event of an operating system crash. You can use System Center Data Protection Manager to provide a full backup of the operating system. A best practice is to perform a monthly operating system backup of all the Configuration Manager site server systems.

Another best practice is to perform regular database backups of the Configuration Manager database. This backup can be used to restore Configuration Manager. Database backups are useful because they can be compressed, which saves disk space, and Configuration Manager services are not affected when a database backup is performed.

Restoring Configuration Manager

Restoring is only possible if you have already backed up the Configuration Manager information. The most common scenarios where you might want to recover Configuration Manager are:

- A site server operating system crash.
- A Configuration Manager functional crash.
- Hardware replacement.
- An OS upgrade of the server on which Configuration Manager is installed. This is not applicable to in-place OS upgrades, except for an in-place update from Server 2012 to Server 2012 R2.

Recovering from a site server operating system crash

When a server operating system crashes, the first thing you have to do is to perform a restore from a backup. After installing the operating system, you can continue with the steps required to restore it from a Configuration Manager functional crash.

Recovering from a Configuration Manager functional crash

In this scenario, Configuration Manager is no longer functional. You can use the Configuration Manager setup program to recover the Configuration Manager environment. Start the setup program by starting the Configuration Manager setup and perform the following steps:

1. On the first page of the wizard, you need to verify all the prerequisites and then click on **Next**.
2. The **Available Setup Options** page includes all the options you can initiate when running the setup, as follows:
    - Install a Configuration Manager primary site

- ○ **Install a Configuration Manager central administration site**
- ○ **Upgrade an existing Configuration Manager 2012 installation**
- ○ **Recover a site**
- ○ **Perform site maintenance or reset this site**
- ○ **Uninstall a Configuration Manager site**

3. Some of these options are greyed out depending on the state of the computer on which the setup program is started. Select **Recover a site** and click on **Next**.

4. On the next page, the **Site Server and Database Recovery** option lists all the possible recovery options. Select **Recover the site server from an existing backup** and click on **Browse** to select the folder containing the Configuration Manager backup. At the bottom of the page, you can choose from the following options:

   - ○ **Recover the site database using the backup set at the following location**
   - ○ **Use existing manually recovered database**

   You can also skip the database recovery step.

5. If the site that you restored is a standalone primary site, you don't need to specify anything in the **Site Recovery Information** page. You can specify a reference site if the site is a central administration site.

6. The **Site and Installation Settings** page contains information taken from the backup files. During the restore of the site, we can choose to restore the Configuration Manager console by checking **Install the Configuration Manager Console**. Click on **Next** to continue.

7. The **Database Information** page contains information taken from the backup files.

8. On the **Settings Summary** page, you can see a summary of the wizard's configuration. Click on **Next** to start the restore process.

9. The wizard automatically runs the prerequisites checker and displays the results on the **Prerequisite check** page. Select **Begin Install** in order to start the recovery process.

10. After the prerequisites check is complete, the actual process begins. The restore can take some time, depending on the size of the database.

11. You might need to perform additional tasks after the restore finishes. The actions are saved to `C:\ConfigMgrPostRecoveryActions.html`.

After restoring a site, you have to examine the Configuration Manager site's status, status messages, and the event log to verify that no errors occurred and that the restored site is functioning normally.

Using backup and restore to migrate to a new environment

You can use the backup and restore process to move your existing Configuration Manager environment to a new hardware or to build a new environment.

Moving Configuration Manager to a new hardware

The general steps that you need to perform in order to migrate Configuration Manager to a new hardware are as follows:

1. Backup the existing Configuration Manager. When the backup is done, shut down the server.

2. Install a new server with the same server name, domain membership, partitions, and configuration.

3. Restore Configuration Manager.

Building a new Configuration Manager environment

Sometimes, you might need to build a new Configuration Manager environment and replace the existing one. This can happen if a Configuration Manager server cannot retain the same name and needs to be moved to a new hardware.

 You cannot change the name of the server or the domain membership if Configuration Manager is installed.

The new environment might also be required when too many issues exist in the current Configuration Manager environment. The high-level steps that you need to perform are the following:

1. Install a new Configuration Manager server using a different site code from the previous one.

2. Set Configuration Manager's server environment to the settings you require, including Active Directory System Discovery. Set the site boundaries to overlap with the original Configuration Manager environment. The overlapping of site boundaries is only supported for content location boundary groups and not for site assignments.

3. When all the systems are listed in the **All Systems** collection, right-click on the collection and select **Install Client** to deploy the client to the collection.

4. You can export objects from the old site and import them to the new site if needed.

Summary

This chapter describes the infrastructure security for Configuration Manager and the delegation of administrative access. The chapter included a detailed description of a new role-based administration model and an overview of the Configuration Manager controls and security accounts. The chapter also provided considerations for securing the hierarchy design, audit support and server configurations, and placement. In the second part of the chapter, we saw the required steps to back up, recover, and maintain our Configuration Manager environment.

In the next chapter, we will discuss how to troubleshoot common issues such as server or client malfunctions, network communication problems, or incorrect permissions.

8
Troubleshooting

After the successful installation and configuration of System Center Configuration Manager, you have to design proper administrative tasks and resolve any issues that occur. Maintaining a functional Configuration Manager hierarchy is very important. In this chapter, we will take a look at some of the troubleshooting actions that you can perform when something is not functioning properly in your Configuration Manager infrastructure.

Troubleshooting network issues

For Configuration Manager to work properly, it depends on basic network services, network connectivity, and name resolution. Network-related issues are a common source of problems for Configuration Manager services. You have to keep an open mind when troubleshooting Configuration Manager issues because sometimes, an incorrect security setting can have the same symptoms as a network problem. The following are the common network-related issues that affect Configuration Manager:

- Network configuration issues
- Network connectivity issues
- Name resolution issues
- Blocked or unresponsive ports
- Timeout issues

Network configuration issues

If, by any chance, you suspect that the network configuration of some of your systems is not properly configured, you can log on to the system, open the command prompt, and enter the following command:

```
ipconfig /all
```

You will see a list of all the installed network adapters and their IP addresses. If you cannot see an IP address or if all the IP addresses have an autoconfigured IP address or **Automatic Private IP Addressing (APIPA)** addresses, then something is not configured properly. If this scenario occurs when the server obtains an address from a DHCP server, it means that the server cannot contact the DHCP server. If you have entered multiple IP addresses
on the server, then you can perform tests for the overall TCP/IP stack functionalities by opening the command prompt and entering:

- Ping 127.0.0.1 or
- Ping <IP address of the server>

In both the scenarios, you should see replies in the command line as shown here (if the ICMP traffic is not blocked by the firewall):

```
Reply from 127.0.0.1: bytes=32 time=9ms TTL=128
```

If you receive a request timeout message, then the TCP/IP networking is not working properly.

Troubleshooting connectivity issues

Connectivity problems can occur if:

- Servers do not have a physical connection
- A hardware or a software problem exists on some of the servers or on the intermediate devices, such as switches and routers
- Packets are not properly routed between the servers

To start troubleshooting connectivity issues, log on to one of the affected servers and start pinging the server or the client that it has problems communicating with. To do this, open the command prompt and enter:

```
Ping <IP address of the target server or client>
```

Sometimes, it is better to ping the server or clients' default gateway and see whether you get a response before pinging the actual server or client. In most cases, you will receive a response from the target server or client indicating the time it took to get a reply for the ping. If the server doesn't respond, then you will receive some messages as follows:

- **Request Timed Out**: This message indicates that you haven't got a response in the expected time. In most cases, this is a firewall issue and the server is not configured to respond to ping requests. To check whether the target server is functioning properly, log on to it and ping its own IP address.

- **Destination Host Unreachable or Destination Network Unreachable**: This message is generated by the router, and it indicates that the router has no route to the target server.

Other return values are also possible. For more information, follow this link:

`http://technet.microsoft.com/en-us/library/cc732509.aspx`

You can also use the `tracert` and `pathping` commands to troubleshoot deeper. For more information about these commands, follow this link:

`http://technet.microsoft.com/library/Cc940095`

Name resolution issues

Most of the Configuration Manager components rely on the DNS server for name resolution. To test whether the name resolution is working properly, enter the following in the command prompt:

- Ping <FQDN of the target server>

  For example: `ping server01.home.in`

- Ping <hostname>

  For example: `ping server01`

In each scenario, you will get a response displaying the IP address of the target system, such as:

`Pinging server01.home.in [192.168.1.100] with 32 bytes of data`

If the DNS name resolution fails, you can troubleshoot with the `NSlookup` command. You can get more information about this command at `http://support.microsoft.com/kb/200525`.

Blocked or unresponsive ports

A common source of connectivity problems is blocked ports on some intermediate devices, such as a router or firewall. To troubleshoot problems with specific ports, you can use the `telnet` command to connect to the specific port on the target system. For example, in order to verify that you can connect to the HTTP service (port 80), open the command prompt and enter:

```
telnet <IP address or host name> 80
```

If telnet is successful, you will receive the telnet screen with a cursor. If telnet is not successful, you will receive an error message.

When the connection to a specific port fails, you must first verify that the service is up and is listening on a specific port. On the system that should receive connections, open the command prompt and enter:

```
Netstat -a
```

This will display all the active ports and connections. If the port is not shown in the list, verify that the service is installed and configured. If you can see the port in the list, check the firewall logs for dropped packets.

To test the client's connectivity to an MP server, enter the following URLs in the client's web browser:

- `http://< MP >/sms_mp/.sms_aut?mplist`
- `http://< MP >/sms_mp/.sms_aut?mpcert`
- `https://< MP >/sms_mp/.sms_aut?mplist`
- `https://< MP >/sms_mp/.sms_aut?mpcert`

In order to initiate an HTTPS request to the management point server, you first need to import a certificate into the server if there isn't any.

Timeout issues

The response time that you see from the ping command can help you to confirm network performance problems that could be causing connections to time out. In some cases, timeouts are configurable. However, if timeouts occur frequently, you should review your server placement and network configuration to see whether improvements are possible.

Identifying network issues

All the Configuration Manager functionalities depend on properly configured network services. Here, we will take a look at the services that are most often affected by network issues. These services are site system, client installation, software distribution, and data synchronization in the hierarchy. The following section describes the indicators of the possible network issues that you can see in the status messages and logs. You can use this information for the proactive monitoring of Configuration Manager.

Network issues affecting the site configuration

If there is a problem with the installation or configuration of a site system, it will generally show in the distribution manager status. To view this, go to the **Monitoring** section of the Configuration Manager console and navigate to **System Status | Component Status**. Then, right-click on **SMS_DISTRIBUTION_ MANAGER** and navigate to **View Messages | All**. Here, you can enter the time period in which you want to view messages.

Network issues affecting the client installation

When you have enabled the client push installation or initiated a manual client push, the client Configuration Manager component on the site server is responsible for installing the client on the systems targeted by the installation. If the installation fails, a client configuration request or a .ccr file is moved to the <Configuration Manager Install Path>\inboxes\ccrretry.box folder. A client installation might take more than one attempt to finish. If there are a large number of files in this folder, it might indicate a problem. Problems will also show up under the status for client Configuration Manager. To view this, go to the **Monitoring** workspace of the console and navigate to **System Status | Component Status**. Then, right-click on **SMS_CLIENT_CONFIG_MANAGER**.

Issues with the Service Principal Name

The **Service Principal Name (SPN)** provides information that is used by clients to identify and mutually authenticate with other services using the Kerberos authentication. Services use the Active Directory SPN registration to provide information to clients. If the SPN registration is incorrect or missing, it can cause problems with client communication with site systems. In order to register the SPN, you have to do the following:

- If you have a SQL Server service that is running under a domain account on the site database server, use the instructions at this link:

  `http://technet.microsoft.com/en-us/library/hh427336.aspx#BKMK_ManageSPNforDBSrv`

  If the SQL Server service is running under the local system account, you don't have to manually register the SPN.

- If the site system requires an IIS server and if the system is registered in the DNS using a CNAME rather than an A record, you have to register the SPN using the procedure described at this link:

  `http://support.microsoft.com/kb/929650/en-us`

Network issues affecting the software distribution

Software distribution relies on a properly configured and functional network to send content to distribution points and on clients to download content from distribution points. You can find information about the functioning of content deployment in the **Monitoring** section of the Configuration Manager console in the distribution status node. You can view the distribution status messages in the **SMS_DISTRIBUTION_MANAGER** component in **Component Status** under **System Status**. You can find additional details in the `Distmgr.log` file. If it is a remote distribution point, you will have to look for details in the `pkgxfemgr.log` file, or if it is a pull distribution point, the `PullDP.log` file.

Your network topology might change over time. You might add more IP subnets, or you might change the IP addressing. It is important to modify the Configuration Manager boundaries and boundary groups to reflect these changes. If you fail to update Configuration Manager boundaries and boundary groups, then it might cause problems with the software distribution.

Network issues affecting site communications

Site-to-site communication problems can cause problems such as the replication of objects from parent to child sites or data from the child site not being updated on the parent site. The details about problems with site communication are stored as files in these folders:

- `<Configuration Manager Install Path>\inboxes\schedule.box\outboxes\<sender name>`

  If there are a lot of files in this folder, then the sender will have problems processing requests or the sender will experience problems while connecting to another site

- `<Configuration Manager Install Path>\inboxes\schedule.box\ requests`

  This folder stores send requests before sending them to the sender

- `<Configuration Manager Install Path>\inboxes\schedule.box\ tosend`

  This folder stores the package and instruction files to be transferred to another site

If you see a lot of files in any of these folders, then immediately check the sender log on the sending site (`sender.log`). Or, if it is the receiving site, then you have to check `despool.log`. You can also view the **SMS_LAN_SENDER** status in the Configuration Manager console. You will find it in the **Monitoring** section by going to **System Status | Component Status**.

Troubleshooting the data replication service

For site-to-site communication, System Center Configuration Manager uses the SQL Service Broker to replicate data between site databases instead of file-based replication, as it was done in the previous versions. SQL replication improves both performance and reliability. However, it might be more difficult to troubleshoot a replication issue.

To view the status of the replication, open the Configuration Manager console and navigate to **Monitoring | Overview | Site Hierarchy**. Additionally, Configuration Manager can perform file-based replication for some of the Configuration Manager data. The following table shows which data is replicated by SQL replication and which is replicated by file-based replication:

Data type	Example	Replication type	Data location
Global data	<ul><li>Collection rules</li><li>Metadata for packages</li><li>Metadata for software updates</li><li>Deployments</li></ul>	SQL replication	<ul><li>CAS</li><li>Primary sites</li><li>Secondary sites</li></ul>
Site data	<ul><li>Collection members</li><li>Alert messages</li></ul>	SQL replication	<ul><li>CAS</li><li>Originating Primary site</li></ul>

Data type	Example	Replication type	Data location
Content	<ul><li>Software packages</li><li>Software updates</li><li>Boot images</li></ul>	File-based replication	<ul><li>Primary site</li><li>Secondary site</li><li>Distribution point</li></ul>

To troubleshoot issues for the data replication service, follow the guidelines provided at the following link:

```
http://blogs.msdn.com/b/minfangl/archive/2012/05/16/tips-for-
troubleshooting-sc-2012-configuration-manager-data-replication-
service-drs.aspx
```

Troubleshooting console issues

The new role-based Configuration Manager console is a great option when you want to give permissions to users. Problems can occur if users are given wrong permissions. They often occur when insufficient and sometimes inappropriate security permissions have been assigned. In the upcoming topics, we will take a look at some of the most common issues that occur and how to resolve them.

Console logging

Configuration Manager provides rich and detailed logs for all the events that occur in the Configuration Manager infrastructure. The Configuration Manager console provides the same rich and detailed logging of all the events. You can view the log and gain an insight on what was happening in Configuration Manager. You can find the logs in the `SMSAdminUI.log` file that is located at `<%ProgramFiles%>\Microsoft Configuration Manager\AdminConsole\AdminUILog`. The default logging level doesn't provide much detail. You can enable verbose logging by navigating to `<%ProgramFiles%>\Microsoft Configuration Manager\AdminConsole\bin`. When you get to the folder, you have to do the following:

1. Open the file named `Microsoft.ConfigurationManagement.exe.config`.

2. Search for the line `<source name="SmsAdminUISnapIn" switchValue="Error">` and change the value of `"Error"` to `"Verbose"`.

3. Restart the Configuration Manager console, if it is open, for the setting to take effect.

If you have verbose logging enabled, the log size and the write operations increase. Monitor the hard disk space if the log increases.

Verifying WMI permissions

To validate **Windows Management Instrumentation** (**WMI**) permissions, you must check two different WMI namespaces. The namespaces are along the same path, but the privileges for each namespace differ and that is why the child namespace does not inherit from the parent. The following screenshots show you how to give access to a local group. To verify WMI permissions, you have to do the following:

1. On the site server, start the **Component Services** console. To do this, go to the Start icon, click on **Administrative Tools**, and select **Computer Management**.

2. Expand the **Services and Application** node and right-click on **WMI Control**.

3. From the menu, select **Properties** to launch the WMI control properties, as shown in the following screenshot:

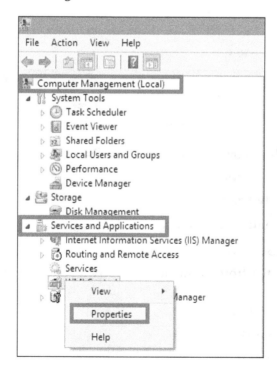

4. Switch to the **Security** tab and expand the **Root** node. Select **SMS** and click on the **Security** button, as shown here:

5. Verify that the following permissions are listed:
    ° **Enable Account**
    ° **Remote Enable**

6. Expand the **SMS** node and select **site_<site code>_node**.

7. Click on the **Security** button.

8. Select **Properties** from the menu and verify that the following permissions are listed:
    ° **Enable Account**
    ° **Execute Methods**
    ° **Provider Writer**
    ° **Remote Enable**

9. Close all the dialog windows.

Verifying DCOM permissions

The minimum required **Distributed Component Object Model (DCOM)** permission is Remote Activation. To verify Remote Activation permissions, you have to perform the following steps:

1. On the site server, start the **Component Services** console. Go to the Start button, click on **Run**, and then type `dcomcnfg.exe`.

2. Expand **Component Services**, then expand **Computers**, and click on **My Computer**.

3. Right-click on **My Computer** and select **Properties** from the menu, as shown here:

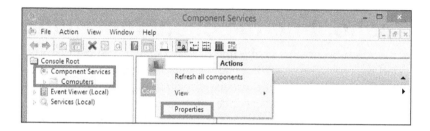

4. Switch to the **COM Security** tab.

5. In the lower section of the page where it says **Launch and Activation Permissions**, click on **Edit Limits...**. If the permissions are in order, the following steps are not needed:

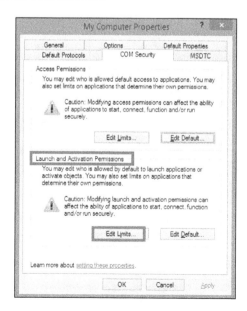

6. Click on **Add** and specify the interested account or group. After this, click on **OK**.

7. In the permission area, only select **Remote Activation**; everything else should be deselected.

8. Click on **OK** to close the **Launch and Activation permissions** dialog window, and again click on **OK** to close the **My Computer Properties** dialog window.

9. All other values in the permission area are deselected; only select **Remote Activation**.

10. Close the Component Services console.

Troubleshooting the client installation

A client installation might cause problems for many reasons; this depends on how you install the client, whether the client can be reached, and whether all the prerequisite software is installed. When you use a client push, ensure that all the prerequisites are fulfilled, the site server can connect to the client machines, and that one of the configured client push installation accounts has permissions to the ADMIN$ share on the target machine. Some of the common issues when Configuration Manager cannot connect to the client are:

- Incorrect firewall configuration

- The ADMIN$ share is not available

- The client push installation account is locked out, or the password has expired

- There is a pending reboot that is initiated by another software, which prevents the installation of the Configuration Manager client

- A corrupted DCOM or WMI configuration

You can find more articles on troubleshooting the Configuration Manager client installation at the following sites:

- http://blogs.technet.com/b/sudheesn/archive/2010/05/31/ troubleshooting-sccm-part-i-client-push-installation.aspx

- http://blogs.technet.com/b/configmgrteam/archive/2009/05/08/ wmi-troubleshooting-tips.aspx

If the site server connects to the client, the site server copies all the necessary files to the `%windir%\ccmsetup` folder and starts the installation from here. From this point onward, you can follow the installation progress in the `ccmsetup.log` file. The logfile provides detailed information about each step taken by the `CCMSetup.exe` executable, providing information about what went wrong if the client doesn't install successfully. Problems can be caused by incorrectly configured site boundaries and boundary groups or `ccmsetup bootstrapper` being unable to find the necessary files to install the software prerequisites from the management point. The management point is used as a fallback source only, and binaries are downloaded from a distribution point. Configuration Manager provides reports to assist you with failing client installations; you can proceed with the following steps:

1. In the **Monitoring** section of the console, navigate to **Overview** | **Reporting** | **Reports** | **Client Push**.

2. You can see several reports that are available, regarding client push installations:

    ○   Client push installation's status details

    ○   Client push installation's status details for a specified site

    ○   Client push installation's status summary

    ○   Client push installation's status summary for a specified site

3. Select one of the reports and click on **Run** from the ribbon to open a page where you can provide criteria for the report.

4. This report will provide guidance on where the client push installation failed and where you should investigate.

Troubleshooting compliance settings

Troubleshooting compliance settings is largely a logfile review exercise. Because the evaluation of compliance settings is a client activity, the logs for compliance settings processing are on the client site in the client logs folder, which is located in the `%SystemRoot%\CCM\Logs` folder. There are five log files used for compliance settings to store activity. They are:

*   `Ciagent.log`: This file provides information about downloading, storing, and accessing assigned configuration baselines

*   `CITaskManager.log`: This file records information about the configuration item's task scheduling

- `Dcmagent.log`: This file provides high-level information about the evaluation of the assigned configuration baselines plus information regarding compliance settings processes

- `DCMReporting.log`: This file records information about the reporting policy platform results in state messages for the configuration items

- `DcmWmiProvider.log`: This file records information about reading a configuration item with WMI

To see the full list of server and client logfiles in System Center Configuration Manager, follow this link:

`http://blogs.msdn.com/b/lxchen/archive/2009/04/03/a-list-of-sccm-log-files.aspx`

Issues involving the ability of Configuration Manager to evaluate a baseline or configuration item are reported through the Configuration Manager status message reporting mechanism. To view these status messages, perform the following steps:

1. Go to the **Monitoring** section of the Configuration Manager console.

2. Expand **System Status** in the navigation tree and select **Status Message Queries**.

3. From the list of status message queries on the right, select **All Status Messages** and then select **Show Messages** from the ribbon, or right-click on the context menu. If you are running a large Configuration Manager environment, then returning a great number of results from the **All Status Messages** query can take a long time.

4. In the **All Status Messages** dialog window, enter the timeframe for which you want to see the status messages.

Troubleshooting application deployments

Most of the troubleshooting tasks for different Configuration Manager deployments occur in the **Monitoring** section of the Configuration Manager console. Go to the **Monitoring** section and then select **Deployments** from the pane on the left-hand side. You can right-click on the header and go to **Group By** | **Feature Type** in order to organize this view by feature.

Summary information can give you a great overview of the deployment status. It displays the content status, deployment rules, and the created and modified dates for the software, all in one integrated view. Links to related objects are included, which quickly take you to other parts of the console.

If you click on the **Deployment Types** tab at the bottom of the console, you will see the status of the deployment types for all applications. If you click on **View Status** in the **Summary** page, it will display the **Deployment Status** page. This page provides a great amount of detail regarding the deployment. You can click on **Refresh** to see the updated version of the summary or click on **Run Summarization** to manually start the summarization process.

Troubleshooting software updates

The software update process might crash at multiple points. There are many Configuration Manager components that work together to ensure that the process is executed normally. When something goes wrong, it is important to trace where the process broke. Depending on the exact failure point, you can review different logfiles for error messages. To learn more about troubleshooting software updates, you can view the following links:

- http://blogs.msdn.com/b/steverac/archive/2011/04/10/software-updates-internals-mms-2011-session-part-i.aspx

- http://blogs.msdn.com/b/steverac/archive/2011/04/16/software-updates-internals-mms-2011-session-part-ii.aspx

- http://blogs.msdn.com/b/steverac/archive/2011/04/30/software-updates-internals-mms-2011-session-part-iii.aspx

Windows Server Update Services and Software Update Point

The first component in software updates is **Windows Server Update Services** (**WSUS**). It is important because it collects all the information about the available updates. It is used by clients to scan for updates. Configuration Manager will take control over WSUS by implementing the **Software Update Point** (**SUP**). There are three log files for WSUS and SUP, which are located in the <Configuration Manager Install Path>\Logs folder. They are:

- WCM.log: This file provides information about the SUP configuration and connecting to the WSUS server for subscribed update categories, classification, and languages

- WSUSCtrl.log: This file provides information about the configuration, database connectivity, and health of the WSUS server for the Configuration Manager site

- Wsyncmgr.log: This file provides information about the software updates' synchronization process

Most of the errors that occur with WSUS are configuration errors, including not matching the ports configured during the installation of WSUS and then configured in the SUP. Also, some common issues are Internet connectivity issues because of the firewall, proxy servers, or some other intermediate devices. You must check whether the WSUS server has Internet connectivity.

Troubleshooting SQL Server Reporting Services

After the installation and configuration of **SQL Server Reporting Services (SSRS)**, it is generally trouble-free. Sometimes, you must check and diagnose the correct issues that can occur. There are two areas where you have to investigate issues within SSRS. These are logfiles and event error logs.

SSRS uses a great number of logfiles, which are native to SSRS and some are generated with the interaction with Configuration Manager:

- **SQL Server's report server log files**: You can find more information on these files at `http://msdn.microsoft.com/en-us/library/ms157403.aspx`

- **Report server service trace log**: These files are created daily and contain detailed information

- **Report server execution log**: This is a diagnostic log that you can enable in the reporting site settings

- **Report server HTTP log**: This is a diagnostic log that can be enabled by modifying the `ReportServerService.exe` configuration file

- **Srsrpsetup.log**: This is a Configuration Manager SSRS reporting point installation log

- **SrsrpMSI**: This is a Configuration Manager SSRS MSI-based installation log file

- **Srsrp.log**: These log files contains the Configuration Manager SSRS logging together with real-time reporting information

- **Windows application log**: This log includes event logging and can indicate potential errors in SSRS

If you want to see the full error list that SSRS can generate, follow this link:

`http://msdn.microsoft.com/en-us/library/ms165307.aspx`

Summary

This chapter presented the different aspects of how to troubleshoot issues regarding the functionalities of Configuration Manager. It began with common network-related issues and then continued by explaining common Configuration Manager console issues. Then it provided information on how to troubleshoot client installations, client compliance settings, and application deployment. At the end, there was a section on how to troubleshoot software updates and SQL Server Reporting Services.

Index

enrollment point 160
enrollment proxy point 161

F

fallback status point 160
features, Endpoint Protection
  customizable 57
  licensing 57
  separate client 58
filesystem-based detection method
  creating 112

G

global conditions
  about 101
  using 101

H

hardware inventory device settings 177-179
heartbeat method 158
hierarchy
  maintaining 42
  monitoring 41
hierarchy planning
  about 158
  Central Administration Site (CAS) 159
  Configuration Manager sites 159
  primary site 159
  secondary site 159
hierarchy-specific configurations
  boundaries 41
  boundary groups 41
  client settings 41
  resource discovery 41
  role-based authentication 41
hierarchy-wide roles, deploying on CAS
  reporting services point 161
  system health validator point 161
hierarchy-wide site system roles
  about 160
  asset intelligence synchronization point 160
  Endpoint Protection point 160
  top-level software update point 160
HTTPS
  advantages 221

I

IDMIF files 178
in-console alerts 168
installation methods, Configuration
    Manager client agent
  client push installation 164
  group policy installation 165
  logon script installation 165
  manual installation 164
  software update point based
      installation 164
  upgrade installation 165
interactive features, of reporting services
  actions 148
  document maps 148
  interactive sorting 148
  report parameters 148
  subreport 148
Internet Information Services (IIS) 216

L

local administration, site system
  audit account management category 220
  audit object access category 220
  audit policy change category 220
  securing 220

M

malware
  details, monitoring 79
  Endpoint Protection details, monitoring 79
  on-demand actions, performing 80
  remediation status 79
  top malware 79
management point 160
Man in the middle 221
Microsoft application virtualization
    deployment type 100
Microsoft Report Builder 140
Microsoft tools
  using 56
Microsoft Visual Studio 140
MIF files
  IDMIF 178
  NOIDMIF 178

Thank you for buying
Mastering System Center
Configuration Manager

About Packt Publishing

Packt, pronounced 'packed', published its first book, *Mastering phpMyAdmin for Effective MySQL Management*, in April 2004, and subsequently continued to specialize in publishing highly focused books on specific technologies and solutions.

Our books and publications share the experiences of your fellow IT professionals in adapting and customizing today's systems, applications, and frameworks. Our solution-based books give you the knowledge and power to customize the software and technologies you're using to get the job done. Packt books are more specific and less general than the IT books you have seen in the past. Our unique business model allows us to bring you more focused information, giving you more of what you need to know, and less of what you don't.

Packt is a modern yet unique publishing company that focuses on producing quality, cutting-edge books for communities of developers, administrators, and newbies alike. For more information, please visit our website at www.packtpub.com.

About Packt Enterprise

In 2010, Packt launched two new brands, Packt Enterprise and Packt Open Source, in order to continue its focus on specialization. This book is part of the Packt Enterprise brand, home to books published on enterprise software – software created by major vendors, including (but not limited to) IBM, Microsoft, and Oracle, often for use in other corporations. Its titles will offer information relevant to a range of users of this software, including administrators, developers, architects, and end users.

Writing for Packt

We welcome all inquiries from people who are interested in authoring. Book proposals should be sent to author@packtpub.com. If your book idea is still at an early stage and you would like to discuss it first before writing a formal book proposal, then please contact us; one of our commissioning editors will get in touch with you.

We're not just looking for published authors; if you have strong technical skills but no writing experience, our experienced editors can help you develop a writing career, or simply get some additional reward for your expertise.

Microsoft System Center Configuration Manager Advanced Deployment

ISBN: 978-1-78217-208-6 Paperback: 290 pages

Design, implement, and configure System Center Configuration Manager 2012 R2 with the help of real-world examples

1. Learn how to design and operate Configuration Manager 2012 R2 sites.

2. Explore the power of Configuration Manager 2012 R2 for managing your client and server estate.

3. Discover up-to-date solutions to real-world problems in System Center Configuration Manager administration.

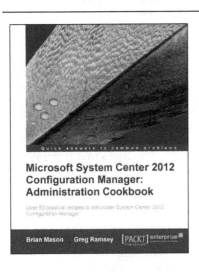

Microsoft System Center 2012 Configuration Manager: Administration Cookbook

ISBN: 978-1-84968-494-1 Paperback: 224 pages

Over 50 practical recipes to administer System Center 2012 Configuration Manager

1. Administer System Center 2012 Configuration Manager.

2. Provides fast answers to questions commonly asked by new administrators.

3. Skip the why's and go straight to the how-to's.

4. Gain administration tips from System Center 2012 Configuration Manager MVPs with years of experience in large corporations.

Please check **www.PacktPub.com** for information on our titles

Microsoft System Center Data
Protection Manager 2012 SP1

ISBN: 978-1-84968-630-3   Paperback: 328 pages

Learn how to deploy, monitor, and administer
System Center Data Protection Manager 2012 SP1

1. Practical guidance that will help you get the
    most out of Microsoft System Center Data
    Protection Manager 2012.

2. Gain insight into deploying, monitoring, and
    administering System Center Data Protection
    Manager 2012 from a team of Microsoft MVPs.

3. Learn the various methods and best practices
    for administrating and using Microsoft System
    Center Data Protection Manager 2012.

System Center 2012 R2 Virtual
Machine Manager Cookbook
Second Edition

ISBN: 978-1-78217-684-8   Paperback: 428 pages

Over 70 recipes to help you design, configure, and
manage a reliable and efficient virtual infrastructure
with VMM 2012 R2

1. Create, deploy, and manage data centers
    and private and hybrid clouds with hybrid
    hypervisors using VMM 2012 R2.

2. Integrate and manage fabric (compute,
    storages, gateways, and networking), services
    and resources, and deploy clusters from bare
    metal servers.

Please check **www.PacktPub.com** for information on our titles

www.ingramcontent.com/pod-product-compliance
Lightning Source LLC
Chambersburg PA
CBHW060528060326
40690CB00017B/3423